TABLE OF CONTENTS

Introduction 1

Strategic Communication Defined 4

Strategic Communication as a Shaping Operation 8

Five Evaluation Criteria of Effective Strategic Communication.......................... 12

    Context 13

    Content 16

    Coordination 17

    Delivery 18

    Assessment 19

    An Example of Ineffective Strategic Communication: Disbanding the Iraqi Army 20

Context and Future of the Conflict in Colombia 23

Applying "Context" Criterion to U.S. Strategic Communication Efforts 32

    Structuring the Issue: The FARC as Terrorists 33

    Leveraging the System: Supporting the Colombian Solution 40

Applying "Coordination" Criterion to U.S. Strategic Communication Efforts................ 43

Conclusion.. 49

Recommendations 52

Bibliography... 57

Introduction

"A more peaceful, just, and stable Colombia is undoubtedly in our national interest."
                                                    - Senator Barack Obama, 8 March 2007[1]

Colombia's future hangs in the balance with dire implications for Latin America and U.S. national interests. After almost forty-five years of existential conflict, Colombia has the opportunity to be the "peaceful, just, and stable" country that President Obama described. With rising anti-American sentiment in South America, securing Colombia is essential for regional stability and U.S. national interests.[2] Years of fierce and bloody fighting and a billion U.S. dollars later, the Colombian government has the *Fuerzas Armadas Revolucionarias de Colombia* (FARC), or the Revolutionary Armed Forces of Colombia, on the ropes. The FARC, a social revolutionary and narco-terrorist group who is Colombia's greatest organized threat, is seriously weakened and faces open opposition and isolation from the Colombian populace and the international community.[3] The FARC's defeat is critical to increase Colombia's stability. However, the group's communist roots enable it to regain sufficient traction in a country with the socio-economic conditions fertile for leftist ideology. Therefore, action needs to be taken and continued to ensure the long-term decline of the FARC. Given Colombia's strategic importance

---

[1] Senator Barack Obama, speaking on President George H.W. Bush's trip to Latin America, on March 8, 2007, Cong. Rec., 110th Cong., 1st sess., 2007: S2896.

[2] The negative effects of Colombia's conflict on regional security and U.S. national interests is cited in numerous sources. See Thomas A. Marks, "A Model Counterinsurgency: Uribe's Colombia (2002-2006) vs FARC," *Military Review* (March-April 2007): 56; Craig Arcenaux and David Pion-Berlin, *Transforming Latin America: The International and Domestic Origins of Change* (Pittsburgh: University of Pittsburgh Press, 2005), 200; Kim Cragin and Bruce Hoffman, *Arms Trafficking and Colombia* (Santa Monica: RAND, 2003), xxi; Gabriel Marcella, *War Without Borders: The Colombian-Ecuador Crisis of 2008* (Carlisle: Strategic Studies Institute, 2008).

[3] Dr. Gabriel Marcella, former professor at the U.S. Army War College and International Affairs Advisor to the Commander of U.S. Southern Command, described the FARC as "the main insurgent group that contests the government for territorial control and authority...." Gabriel Marcella, *American Grand Strategy for Latin America in the Age of Resentment* (Carlisle: Strategic Studies Institute, 2007), 36; See also Jane's Information Group, "Security, Colombia," Jane's Security Sentinel Security Assessment, December 11, 2008, www.janes.com (accessed February 5, 2009); Peter Deshazo, Tanya Primiani, and Phillip McLean, *Back from the Brink: Evaluating Progress in Colombia, 1999-2007* (Washington, DC: Center for Strategic and International Studies, 2007), viii.

and historic position as an ally in the region, the U.S. needs to continue support for the government's operations against the FARC. As Colombia's operations transition from military to policing, U.S. support is most needed in strategic communication efforts.

Effective strategic communication is vital in shaping the FARC's long-term decline. Maintaining popular support and insurgent-population isolation, prerequisites for any successful counterinsurgency, is the priority for the Colombian government.[4] To achieve these ends, Colombia's government should progress along important, simultaneous lines of efforts. The government needs to address the basis of a social revolutionary cause, such as poverty, inequitable distribution of wealth, unemployment, and legitimate governance to maintain credibility among the people. Reinforcing these efforts, however, requires an effective strategic communication campaign to persuade the population that continued support for the government is the right choice.[5] Effective strategic communication also degrades the FARC's cause and activities in the eyes of the Colombian people and the international community.[6] Over time, the population isolates itself from the FARC, which is necessary for the narco-terrorist's defeat.[7] In

---

[4] Popular support for the counterinsurgent and population-insurgent isolation are necessary for a successful counterinsurgency and counterterrorism. See David Galula, *Counterinsurgency Warfare: Theory and Practice.* (1964; repr., St. Petersburg: Hailer Publishing, 2005), 74-78; Sir Robert Thompson, *Defeating Communist Insurgency: The Lessons of Malaya and Vietnam* (1966: repr., St. Petersburg: Hailer Publishing, 2005), 51; Bard O'Neill, *Insurgency & Terrorism: From Revolution to Apocalypse*, 2nd ed. (Dulles: Potomac Books, 2005), 169; U.S. Department of the Army, *Field Manual 3-24: Counterinsurgency* (Washington, D.C.: December 2006), 1-3; Jeremy M. Weinstein, *Inside Rebellion: The Politics of Insurgent Violence*, Cambridge Studies in Comparative Studies (New York: Cambridge University Press, 2007), 29; Jerrold M. Post, *The Mind of the Terrorist: The Psychology of Terrorism from the IRA to al-Qaeda* (New York: Palgrave Macmillan, 2007), 251-252.

[5] Thompson, 65-69. Professor Kenneth Payne is a teaching fellow at the United Kingdom Joint Services Command and Staff College. He writes "Persuading the local audience that your message is credible is the elixir of counterinsurgency." Kenneth Payne, "Waging Communication War," *Parameters* 38, no.2 (Summer 2008): 46.

[6] Many sources highlight the vital importance of strategic communication or similar information operations information in a counterinsurgency or counterterrorism campaign, see Galula, 122; Thompson, 90. O'Neill, 184-185; Payne, 41; Post, 251-252; Seth G. Jones and Martin C. Libicki, *How Terrorist Groups End: Lessons for Countering Al Qaida* (Santa Monica: RAND Corporation, 2008), 135.

[7] Galula writes, "A victory [in counterinsurgency warfare] is that plus the permanent isolation of the insurgent from the population but maintained by and with the population." Galula, 77.

essence, strategic communication shapes the environment so that the FARC's isolation is a long-term consequence. U.S. efforts must empower the Colombians to achieve this end, and effective strategic communication is a requirement for success.

Therefore, it is imperative to assess whether the U.S. is effectively employing strategic communication to shape the long-term decline of the FARC. U.S. strategic communication, a crucial aspect of the information instrument of national power, is central to supporting the Colombian solution, which has led to the FARC's weakened status. To successfully address this question, strategic communication is defined and several key points are highlighted. Next, a discussion of strategic communication's fundamental role and utility as a shaping function in today's information environment is provided. In this particular context, strategic communication is employed as a post-conflict mechanism to shape the long-term decline of an enemy among a population; consequently, strategic communication should be an integral part of the U.S. government's daily operations at all levels. The study then introduces evaluation criteria used to assess the merits of a strategic communication campaign.

To measure effectiveness of U.S. strategic communication efforts, the following five evaluation criteria are presented: *context*, *content*, *coordination*, *delivery,* and *assessment*.[8] Context ensures the communicator has effectively structured the issue and has a systemic understanding of the situation. Content is an assessment of whether the narrative will resonate with the audience. Coordination ensures the actions and words are coordinated and synchronized vertically and horizontally to achieve a synergistic effect. Delivery ensures the methods employed are in line with the context of the environment and accounts for the duration necessary for effect. Finally, assessment ensures that the received messages lead to the anticipated and desired

---

[8] The evaluation criteria proposed are the summarization of a broad base of theory, U.S. policy, opinion of communication experts, and reports from respected non-partisan organizations. The section explaining the criteria provides the supporting evidence. The proposed criteria are important because they assess the complete cycle of a strategic communication campaign, from contextual understanding to measurement and assessment of impacts.

consequences. If not, assessment ensures that feedback mechanisms allow for necessary re-framing of the context or adjustment to content, coordination, or delivery. After review of the evaluation criteria, two of the five, context and coordination, are used to evaluate U.S. strategic communication efforts to assess their effectiveness.

Evaluation of U.S. strategic communication, according to context and coordination, suggests that efforts, in general, are effective at shaping the long-term decline of the FARC. Context analysis suggests the U.S. effectively structured the issue when identifying the FARC as terrorists in 2001. Subsequent U.S. and Colombian government strategic communication has consistently reinforced the appropriate label, thus degrading the FARC's image and delegitimizing its actions for both Colombians and the international community. Ultimately, this has allowed both groups to isolate themselves from the FARC, a prerequisite for its long-term decline. Context analysis also suggests that U.S. understanding of the requirement for a Colombian solution and subsequent efforts to build and support the government's strategic communication capabilities are effective. Coordination analysis suggests that there is effective synchronization below the U.S. national level among the executive agencies and with the Colombian government. However, the lack of a Colombia specific U.S. strategic communication plan at the national level limits synergy of effects, which could be more effective at shaping the long-term decline of the FARC. To understand these conclusions, it is first necessary to define strategic communication.

Strategic Communication Defined

Even though strategic communication is often cited as a key enabler in the modern world, it does not have a commonly accepted definition. There are many useful ones provided by the

Department of Defense (DoD), Department of State (DoS), academia, and the business world. [9]

However, this section introduces the definition proposed in recent Congressional legislation as

the most applicable one to this study and briefly describes why.

The *Strategic Communications Act of 2008*, introduced into the U.S. Senate by Kansas

Senator Sam Brownback defines strategic communication as the following: [10]

> Engaging foreign audiences through coordinated and truthful communications programs
> that create, preserve, or strengthen conditions favorable to the advancement of the
> national interests of the United States. [11]

The bill proposed the establishment of a National Center for Strategic Communication, abolishing

the State Department's Under Secretary for Public Diplomacy and Public Affairs and the

Broadcasting Board of Governors. The purpose of the center is "to advise the President regarding

public diplomacy and international broadcasting to promote democracy and human rights." [12]

The definition incorporates the desired effects of strategic communication, broadly

defines the methods, and clearly distinguishes foreign from U.S. domestic audiences. The

definition is also explicit on key points concerning strategic communication. First, it clearly states

the imperatives for a strategic communication campaign, which are truthful and coordinated.

---

[9] The DoD defines strategic communication as "the focused United States government efforts to understand and engage key audiences to create, strengthen, or preserve conditions favorable to advance national interests and objectives through the use of coordinated information, themes, plans, programs, and actions synchronized with other instruments of national power." U.S. Department of Defense, *Joint Publication 5-0, Joint Operation Planning*. (Washington, DC: December 2006) xii.

[10] The 2008 Strategic Communications Act (S3546) stalled in the U.S. Senate's Committee on Foreign Relations during the 110th Congress in part due to the fact it was introduced so late (September) in the year. According to a Legislative Assistant in Senator Brownback's Washington D.C. office, the goal was "to advance the concept as something worth looking at." Thus, the act effectively died at the initiation of the new Congress. At some point, Senator Brownback plans to plans to re-introduce the bill, incorporating the feedback gained from its original introduction. Phone interview with a Legislative Assistant in Senator Sam Brownback's Washington D.C. Office, March 12, 2009. The name of the interviewee is withheld by mutual agreement. The author advocates the re-introduction and passing of this legislation, which is covered in the recommendation section of this monograph. Support is not universal, even among military. One person in a strategic communication-related capacity interviewed for this study strongly disapproved of the proposal, claiming it was tantamount to micro-management.

[11] *Strategic Communication Act of 2008*, S 3546, 110th Cong., *Congressional Record* (September 23, 2008): S 9283-9284

[12] Ibid.

Truthfulness is, without a doubt, the most crucial element of any strategic communication campaign. Beyond the moral imperative that the U.S. must speak the truth, any perception of dishonestly immediately taints any future engagement as propaganda and negatively affects a government's credibility. [13] Admiral James G. Stavridis, Commander of U.S. Southern Command, writes, "Nothing will more quickly doom strategic communication to failure than even a single instance of falsehood."[14] Establishing truthfulness must be accompanied by effective coordination.

Coordination and synchronization of action and messages is also critical to success in strategic communication.[15] However, this seems to be more problematic at the national level after the abolition of the United States Information Agency (USIA) in 1999. The Foreign Affairs Council argued that public diplomacy is a weakness of the DoS's efforts. The council wrote, "Absent were the detailed annual country communication plans that had been standard until the abolition of the U.S. Information Agency in 1999. Those plans used to cover core messages and themes, target audiences, key opinion leaders, audience attitudes and the local media environment."[16] Another critic is Senator Sam Brownback. While introducing the *Strategic Communication Act of 2008*, Senator Brownback lamented the government's waste of funds and resources. He argued that the public diplomacy and strategic communication actions of the Broadcasting Board of Governors, the State Department and the Department of Defense were

---

[13] Many sources reinforce this point. Thompson, 96.

[14] Admiral James G. Stavridis, "Strategic Communication and National Security," *Joint Force Quarterly,* no. 46 (July, 2007): 5.

[15] Christopher Paul from the RAND Corporation conducted a survey of thirty-six strategic communication proposals and recommendations, including Government Accountability Office reports, U.S. Advisory Commission on Public Diplomacy, Center for Strategic and International Studies, and other recognized subject matter experts. "The need for better coordination and organizational changes (or additions)" was one of the four common themes that emerged, as advocated in nineteen of the reports. Christopher Paul, *Whither Strategic Communication?: A Survey of Current Proposals and Recommendations*, (Santa Monica, RAND Corporation, 2009), 4.

[16] Foreign Affairs Council, *Task Force Report: Managing Secretary Rice's State Department: An Independent Assessment* (Washington, DC: June 2007), 20.

opaque, not properly accounted for, and uncoordinated.[17] Though its track record was not perfect, the USIA, which officially existed from 1953 to 1999, provides examples of where national level synchronization and coordination led to successful strategic communication. An example was USIA's activities after President John F. Kennedy's assassination to introduce President Lyndon B. Johnson to the world. Nicolas Cull, a Professor of Public Diplomacy at the University of Southern California, writes, "In the eight days following Kennedy's death, the USIA's Press Service sent out an unprecedented stream of stories, photographs, briefing papers, and supporting documents: 110 posts in 103 countries received 'material designed to aid understanding and reassurance.'" Cull describes the effects, "USIA surveys of editorial opinion around the world revealed a surge of sympathy for the United States….More importantly, the agency also noted strong approval for Johnson's early statements on foreign policy."[18] Proper coordination is an important criterion for evaluating the effectiveness of strategic communication plan and is covered in more detail later.

Senator Brownback's definition also gives a broader concept of strategic communication, not narrowly defining it as information alone. Coordinated programs need to be multi-faceted, bridging traditional communication techniques with new media. Most important, efforts need to be synchronized with the actions of the government. The employment of strategic communication should be also pervasive, an omnipresent element of U.S. diplomacy, public affairs, and public diplomacy.[19] As Senator Brownback indicated, the effects should shape conditions favorable to U.S. national interests. To accomplish this, strategic communication must be effective in shaping the global environment.

---

[17] *Strategic Communication Act of 2008*, S9284.

[18] Nicolas J. Cull, *The Cold War and the United States Information Agency: American Propaganda and Public Diplomacy, 1945-1989* (New York: Cambridge University Press, 2008), 228-229.

[19] The DoD lists "Pervasive" as one of the Principles of Strategic Communication. U.S. Department of Defense, *Principles of Strategic Communication,* by Robert T. Hastings, Principal Deputy Assistant Secretary of Defense for Public Affairs. (Washington, DC, August 2008).

Strategic Communication as a Shaping Operation

In order to "create, preserve, or strengthen the conditions favorable to the advancement of U.S. national interests," strategic communication should be a routine function of the U.S. government's daily operations. Over time, effective employment of this information instrument of national power, which is well within our current capability, can shape the global environment, both in the media and international public opinion. In today's information age, strategic communication is arguably the most decisive way to do so. This section discusses strategic communication's role as a shaping in influencing foreign audiences and setting conditions favorable for U.S. interests.

Advocates of strategic communication's vital role in foreign policy are not in short supply. For example, a 2009 RAND Corporation report cited thirty-six documents from reputable organizations and over a dozen interviews of subject matter experts.[20] The *2008 National Defense Strategy* described the influence of strategic communication in the future:

> Strategic communications will play an increasingly important role in a unified approach to national security. DoD, in partnership with the Department of State, has begun to make strides in this area, and will continue to do so. However, we should recognize that this is a weakness across the U.S. Government, and that a coordinated effort must be made to improve the joint planning and implementation of strategic communications.[21]

Strategic communication is also recognized outside of Washington. Admiral Stavridis is a staunch believer and practitioner of strategic communication, stressing the requirement for its employment in articles, speeches, and commentary. He writes, "Our approach at U.S. Southern Command is to consider strategic communication as an enabling capability for our policy and

---

[20] Paul, *Whither Strategic Communication?: A Survey of Current Proposals and Recommendations*, v. See also Susan P. Epstein, *Public Diplomacy: A Review of Past Recommendations*. Congressional Research Report for Congress (Washington, DC: September 2005).

[21] U.S. Department of Defense, *National Defense Strategy*, (Washington, D.C: June 2008), 19.

planning decisions and actions."[22] Beyond the U.S., even its avowed enemies attest to the crucial role information has in today's globalized world.

Al Qaeda and other terrorist organizations understand the strategic importance of using the media to shape the environment.[23] The often-cited comment from Al Qaeda's Ayman al-Zawahiri about the "battlefield of the media" inspired terrorists to use new media to extend their influence to non-Arabic speaking American Muslims and the U.S. population as a whole.[24] The purpose is to recruit potential support and influence domestic support for the war effort.[25] In this case, the terrorists are using information to shape the environment for this particular campaign. Subsequently, the U.S. falls into the same pitfall of employing strategic communication only for a specific campaign or action, rather than with a more effective long-term approach guided by a defined strategy.[26]

To effectively shape the environment, strategic communication should go beyond implementation around a significant event, for example, major conflict. It should hold primacy in continuous and routine U.S. efforts to have what the RAND Corporation terms as an "anticipatory shaping" effect. This "anticipatory shaping" effect sets the conditions favorable for U.S. interests, i.e. potentially diffusing problems before they come to a head. This is not a novel concept for the U.S. or its agencies. For example, the RAND report notes, "Several U.S. COCOMs currently

---

[22] Stavridis, "Strategic Communication and National Security," 4.

[23] It is necessary to point out that terrorists are not conducting strategic communication as defined this study due to their frequent lack of truthfulness. They use information as a propaganda tool.

[24] "I say to you: that we are in a battle, and that more than half of this battle is taking place in the battlefield of the media. And that we are in a media battle in a race for the hearts and minds of our Umma." Ayman al-Zawahiri letter to the late Abu Musab al-Zarqawi, who was in charge of Al Qaeda operations in Iraq, July, 9, 2005. Office of the Director of National Intelligence, *Letter from al-Zawahiri to al-Zarqawi*, Press Release, October 11, 2005. http://www.dni.gov/press_releases/20051011_release.htm (accessed October 6, 2008).

[25] Chris Zambelis, "Iraqi Insurgent Media Campaign Targets American Audiences." *Terrorism Focus* 4, no.33 (October 16, 2007), 3.

[26] Stephen Johnson and Helle Dale. *How to Reinvigorate U.S. Public Diplomacy*. Backgrounder #1654. The Heritage Foundation. April 23, 2003, http://www.heritage.org/Research/NationalSecurity/bg1645.cfm, (accessed January 2, 2008).

conduct anticipatory shaping as part of GWOT [Global War on Terror] with the goal of limiting the burgeoning influx of radical ideology and popular support for terrorist organizations."[27] Admiral Stavridis discussed the employment of strategic communication as an anticipatory shaping operation at a Surface Navy Association conference in early 2008. He is quoted, "Our job is not to launch Tomahawk missiles here [in Latin America]. It's effectively to launch ideas....By doing that, maybe you avoid, a decade later the need to be there with a Tomahawk missile."[28] Strategic communication as a shaping operation is also present within U.S. military joint doctrine. In operational phasing, Shape is Phase 0, which occurs prior to and after the implementation of an operational plan. In Phase 0, both military and interagency activities are designed to "dissuade or deter potential adversaries and to assure or solidify relationships with friends or allies....They [the activities] are designed to assure success by shaping perceptions and influencing the behavior of both adversaries and allies."[29] The requirement for pervasive strategic communication activity is evident in concepts that shape the security environment.

Strategic communication is an element of two influential concepts, *Soft Power* and deterrence, which shape the global environment. Former Assistant Secretary of Defense, Joseph S. Nye, advocated shaping world politics in his work on *Soft Power*. According to Nye, soft power "is the ability to get what you want through attraction rather than coercion or payments. It arises from the attractiveness of a country's culture, political ideals, and policies." Commenting on the shaping effect soft power can have, he wrote, "When you can get others to admire your ideals and *to want what you want* [emphasis added], you do not have to spend as much on sticks

---

[27] Todd Helmus, Christopher Paul, and Russell Glenn, *Enlisting Madison Avenue: The Marketing Approach to Earning Popular Support in Theaters of Operation* (Santa Monica: RAND Corporation, 2007), 132.

[28] Grace V. Jean, "U.S. Must Rethink Military Power," *National Defense* 92, no. 655 (June 2008): 28.

[29] U.S. Department of Defense, *Joint Publication 5-0: Joint Operation Planning* (Washington DC: December 2006): IV-35.

and carrots to move them in your direction."[30] However, to achieve the desired effects Nye indicates, soft power via culture, political ideas, and policies must be communicated to international audiences, hence the requirement for strategic communication. Beyond attraction, there is also an element of deterrence, which can have a shaping effect as well. A long-time stalwart of the Cold War, deterrence is built on a solid foundation of strategic communication, for deterrence is ineffective if the threat is not grasped by the target.[31] Since the U.S. remains in a permanent state of deterrence, manifesting itself in some form or another, strategic communication is a decisive tool for the U.S. government to shape the security environment.

Even during times of major conflict, strategic communication has a crucial role. Some military experts argue that strategic communication, in irregular warfare, is the campaign rather than an aspect of it. Retired Marine Corps Colonel T.X. Hammes, suggests that modern insurgencies have become a strategic communication campaign supported by military action.[32] This is a paradigm shift from the traditionally accepted method of conducting operations, which employs strategic communication in support of military operations. Though this point can be reasonably contested, there should be less controversy over strategic communication's role in securing victory after the conflict.

Post-conflict operations require effective strategic communication to shape long-term political arrangements and peace, as is the current situation with Colombia and the FARC. Citing recent events as an example, Joseph Nye wrote, "Winning the peace is harder than winning a war, and soft power is essential to winning the peace."[33] In *The Pursuit of Victory*, Professor of Military History at King's College Brian Bond argued that a statesman needs to preserve political

---

[30] Joseph S. Nye, Jr. *Soft Power: The Means to Succeed in World Politics* (New York: Public Affairs, 2004), x.

[31] Lawrence Freedman. *Deterrence.* (Cambridge: Polity Press, 2004), 28.

[32] Thomas X. Hammes, "The Message is the Insurgency: Strategic Communications in the Society at War" *Marine Corps Gazette* 91, no. 11 (November 2007), 20.

[33] Nye, xii.

control to secure long-term peace after military conflict, which is contingent in part on having to "persuade the beaten enemy to accept the verdict of battle."[34] Another example of strategic communication's role in shaping the post-conflict environment is discussed by Professor John Dower in his Pulitzer Prize Winner *Embracing Defeat: Japan in the Wake of World War II*. He argued "Bridges of Language" manifest in words, slogans, songs, and American-guided radio broadcasts allowed the Japanese to accept defeat, crossing from their past to future.[35] Dower also argued, "SCAP's [Supreme Command for the Allied Powers] war-guilt campaign played an important role in the psychological demilitarization of the Japanese."[36] Employing strategic communication in a post-conflict situation to shape the environment is a decisive element for securing conditions favorable for national interests. Arguably, this is the critical junction at which Colombia is poised, a weakened FARC whose long-term decline can be shaped.

Consequently, to shape an environment requires *effective* strategic communication. Adding to the truthful requirement discussed previously, the next section proposes five evaluation criteria. These criteria can be used to assess the effectiveness of a strategic communication campaign or as it is employed during routine and continuous operations.

Five Evaluation Criteria of Effective Strategic Communication

Drawn from a broad base of theory, including communication, complexity, social science, and social influence analysis, five evaluation criteria are proposed as means to evaluate

---

[34] Brian Bond, *The Pursuit of Victory: From Napoleon to Saddam Hussein* (New York: Oxford University Press, 1996), 5.

[35] John W. Dower, *Embracing Defeat: Japan in the Wake of World War II* (New York: W.W. Norton & Company, 1999), 168-200.

[36] Ibid., 413.

the effective employment of strategic communication.[37] The criteria evaluate the entire cycle of strategic communication, from systemic understanding of the context to assessment. They are the following: context, content, coordination, delivery, and assessment. This section describes the five evaluation criteria.

Context

The most important criterion is context. Properly assessing the context lays the foundation for the strategic communication campaign because it ensures that efforts are relevant to the situation. Therefore, it is imperative that due consideration be given to the context of the situation. There are two aspects to context. The first is how the communicator structures the issue and the resulting identities that are assumed. The second aspect of context is understanding the system in which the issue exists and employing strategic communication in a manner that leverages that understanding.[38]

Structuring the issue during communication is stressed by persuasion theory. The persuasion element has precedent in the work of University of California Professors Anthony Pratkanis and Elliot Aronson. They argue, "Pre-persuasion refers to how the issue is structured and how the decision is framed. If fully successful, pre-persuasion establishes 'what everyone knows' and 'what everyone takes for granted.'"[39] By structuring the debate in an advantageous manner, the communicator directly shapes its outcome. In the same work, they further expand on this concept, "The context they [the 'context-makers'] set can pre-persuade us by influencing our

---

[37] Relevant theories are provided in the descriptions of the evaluation criteria.

[38] Context, as defined by Merriam Webster's Dictionary, has two meanings which are pertinent to this study, "the parts of a discourse that surround a word or passage and can throw light on its meaning" and "the interrelated conditions in which something exists or occur." Merriam-Webster, *Context,* Merriam-Webster Online, http://www.merriam-webster.com/dictionary/context (accessed November 18, 2008).

[39] Anthony Pratkanis and Elliot Aronson, *Age of Propaganda: The Everyday Use and Abuse of Persuasion* (New York: W.H. Freeman, 2001): 51.

perceptions and judgments."[40] In other words, how the communicator structures the debate influences the outcome, often before the debate, itself. Additionally, structuring the debate then can impart identity for the communicator and audience.

Identities and their resulting roles and responsibilities, which develop from the structured debate, impact on the success of strategic communication. In *The Clash of Civilizations and the Remaking of World Order,* Samuel Huntington described the role of identity, "First, everyone has multiple identities which may compete with or reinforce each other: kinship, occupational, cultural, territorial, educational, partisan, ideological, and others." He continues, "Third, identity at any level...can only be defined in relation to an 'other,' a different person, tribe, race, or civilization....Separate codes governed behavior toward those who are 'like us' and the 'barbarians' who are not."[41] Huntington uses "separate codes" that govern behavior to illustrate identities have certain roles and responsibilities. For example, a Colombian population united against self-serving narco-terrorists imparts the responsibility of the former to isolate itself from the latter.

The other element of context is understanding the system in which the issue exists. Understanding the system, or systemic thinking, is essentially an attempt to comprehend the meta-question of *why* something happens.[42] Strategic communication is employed in a complex system, rather than a complicated one, due to the friction caused by the human element.[43]

---

[40] Ibid., 103.

[41] Samuel P. Huntington, *The Clash of Civilizations and the Remaking of World Order* (New York: Simon & Schuster, 1996): 128.

[42] U.S. Army School of Advanced Military Studies, *Art of Design: Student Text,* version 1.0 (Fort Leavenworth, KS: S 2008): 28.

[43] Friction in this context derives from the work of Carl von Clausewitz who argued that each individual "retains his potential of friction." Carl von Clausewitz, *On War*, trans. and ed. Michael Howard and Peter Paret (Princeton: Princeton University Press, 1976), 119.

Complexity theory holds that the essence of complexity is interdependence.[44] Therefore, a systemic understanding must at least analyze its inputs, outputs, behavior of the interdependent parts, and relationships and effects on other systems to be effective.[45] A simple metaphor of systemic thinking is understanding why sounds and melodies are produced by the structure and use of a piano. Taking it a step further, systemic thinking should also assess a system's propensity, or natural tendency, to behave in certain ways.[46] For example, history illustrates that political leadership in Latin America has the natural tendency to be authoritarian in nature, even in a democratic system.[47] To make the leap from theory to system thinking, it often helps to categorize the inputs, outputs, and interdependent parts.

Categorization is a means to start the process of understanding the system. One suggested category is power dynamics, for example, understanding how is it distributed and who and what is in competition for it. Political scientist Colin Gray reveals other categories when examining strategic history. Gray explains that strategic history has seven contexts: political, socio-cultural, economic, technological, military-strategic, geographic, and historical.[48] Another method could be the U.S. military's operational variables, PMESII-PT, which are the following: political, military, economic, social, information, infrastructure, physical environment, and time.[49] Categorization is only a tool for structuring how the system is composed, interacts, and the

---

[44] Dr. Alex Ryan, "Complexity Theory" (lecture, U.S. Army School of Advanced Military Studies, Fort Leavenworth, KS, December 19, 2008). Alex Ryan and Daniel Bilusich, "Complicated or Complex?" (unpublished paper, 2007), 1.

[45] Yaneer Bar-Yam, *Making Things Work: Solving Complex Problem* (Cambridge: Knowledge Press, 2004), 16-19.

[46] U.S. Army School of Advanced Military Studies, 34.

[47] Harry E. Vanden and Gary Prevost, *Politics of Latin America: The Power Game* (New York, Oxford University Press, 2002), 122.

[48] Colin S. Gray, War, Peace, and International Relations: An Introduction to Strategic History (London: Routledge, 2007), 10.

[49] U.S. Department of the Army, *Field Manual 3-0: Operations* (Washington, D.C.: February 2008), 1-5.

resulting effects. Ultimately, the goal is to develop a shared understanding of the system, with strategic communication planners, operational planners, and the leadership.

Proper context allows for strategic communication efforts to be relevant to the situation and provides the foundation upon which to base planning, execution, and assessment. Evaluating strategic communication efforts according to context include answering the following: (1) how has the communicator structured the issue, (2) what identity has the communicator and audience assumed, (3) what are their resulting roles and responsibilities, (4) in what system does the communicator operate or in which the debate is structured, and (5) is the structured issue relevant to the context. The goal is to ensure that strategic communication efforts are synchronized and relevant to the situation. Contextual understanding leads to more effective content.

Content

The second evaluation criterion for evaluating strategic communication is content. According to John Rendon, founder and CEO of The Rendon Group, a global strategic communication firm, "Content is king."[50] For the purposes of this study, there are two aspects of content: audience and message. Proper audience analysis is often the deciding factor in influence campaigns. Admiral Stavridis describes understanding the audience as "the constantly rediscovered golden rule of strategic communication."[51] RAND's "Enlisting Madison Avenue" gives "Know the target audience through segmentation and targeting" as a recommendation for applying commercial marketing practices to shaping operations.[52] Most likely, the audience's context is assessed in the previous criterion. However, audience analysis is a critical step in tailoring the message.

---

[50] John Rendon, "The World, Today and Tomorrow: Past, Present and Future" (lecture, U.S. Army School of Advanced Military Studies, Fort Leavenworth, KS, October 13, 2008). Interview by author, Fort Leavenworth, KS, October 13, 2008.

[51] Stavridis, "Strategic Communication and National Security," 5.

[52] Helmus, Paul, and Glenn, 171.

The other aspect of content is the message. There are many methods to constructing a message, which will resonate with the audience. First, as indicated previously, it must be truthful, for the communicator loses credibility and reliability if not.[53] According to Professors Pratkanis and Aronson, the message should also focus the audience's attention and thoughts on how the communicator has structured the issue. In doing so, the message could distract the audience from arguing against it or even have an element of self-persuasion.[54] The message also needs to be a narrative with a plot that imparts meaning to it.[55] The plot should be built with an understanding of historical, cultural, and linguistic factors, which would impart a meaning that better resonates with the audience. The message should also emphasize the cultural-specific norms, which could serve as deterrents if accepted and internalized by the audience.[56] In general, messages and themes should be generated centrally from the guidance of a higher authority, for example, a National Center for Strategic Communication.[57] Currently, it is possible to derive content from the 2007 U.S. National Strategy for Public Diplomacy and Strategic Communication.[58] Once generated, the dissemination, execution, and assessment should be coordinated.

Coordination

The third criterion is coordination. Coordination vertically to higher authority and horizontally across agencies is crucial for effective strategic communication. In August 2008, the Department of Defense, in concert with other executive agencies, published nine Principles of

---

[53] Stavridis, "Strategic Communication and National Security," 5.

[54] Pratkanis and Aronson, 51.

[55] Hayden White, *The Content of the Form: Narrative Discourse and Historical Representation* (Baltimore: Johns Hopkins University Press, 1987), 2.

[56] Freedman, 4.

[57] Rendon, lecture.

[58] U.S. National Security Council, *U.S. National Strategy for Public Diplomacy and Strategic Communication,* Strategic Communication and Public Diplomacy Policy Coordinating Committee (Washington, DC: 2007).

Strategic Communication. Unity of effort is one of the nine and described as the following, "Strategic communication is a consistent, collaborative process that must be integrated vertically from strategic through tactical levels, and horizontally across stakeholders. Leaders coordinate and synchronize capabilities and instruments of power within their area of responsibility, areas of influence, and areas of interest to achieve desired outcomes."[59] U.S. Army Colonel Jim Marshall, Deputy Director of Strategic Communication for U.S. Southern Command, points out two important considerations for coordination. First, there must be coordination between strategic communication planners and operations planners within an organization. Effective coordination of this type leads to success in his second point. Strategic communication must also reduce the "say-do gap."[60] While reducing the gap between what is said and done should be a result of content planning and production, it is a vital aspect of coordination and delivery as well.

Delivery

The fourth criterion for evaluating strategic communication is delivery. Effective delivery allows for better acceptance of the message. Some experts argue that when using mass media to convey messages, it is important to ensure the delivery is entertaining, does not directly attack the audience's views beliefs or attitudes, and incorporates elements of social marketing or influence.[61] RAND's *Enlisting Madison Avenue* advocates the application of marketing principles to earning popular support in theaters of operations.[62] The report suggests use of social marketing as a method for achieving these ends. The authors write, "Social marketing applies well-grounded

---

[59] U.S. Department of Defense, *Principles of Strategic Communication,* by Robert T. Hastings, Principal Deputy Assistant Secretary of Defense for Public Affairs (Washington, DC, August 2008).

[60] U.S. Army Colonel Jim Marshall, phone interview by author, September 24, 2008. Colonel Marshall first heard the "say-do gap" from Rear Admiral Frank Thorpe, the Chief of Information for the U.S. Navy. "Say-do gap" is also mentioned in the U.S. Department of Defense, *Report of the Defense Science Board: Task Force on Strategic Communication,* (Washington, D.C., 2008).

[61] Pratkanis and Aronson, 283.

[62] Helmus, Paul, and Glenn, title.

commercial marketing techniques to influence noncommercial behavior change in a target audience."[63] Beyond marketing, delivery needs to correlate with the context and content. For example, recognizing that almost 75 percent of the Colombian people on average have a cellular phone versus only 15 percent for phone lines would suggest that a strategic communication effort delivered through cell would be more effective.[64] Finally, delivery must account for the necessary duration of strategic communication efforts to achieve the desired effects of the campaign. Strategic communication campaigns are usually not successful based on one event or message but need to take place over an extended period of time to shape the environment.[65]

Assessment

The final criterion proposed is assessment.[66] Assessment analyzes whether strategic communication achieves its desired consequences and how well adjustments are being made context, content, coordination, or delivery to address any shortfalls. Admiral Stavridis discusses the importance of measurement, "The absolute key to effective communication is rolling out a plan, organizing it widely, executing energetically, and then measuring results."[67] Similarly, the Defense Science Review Board lists "Assess" and "Adapt" as two of the five activities of strategic communication.[68] According to RAND, monitoring and evaluating is a vital step of an

---

[63] Ibid., 113-114. The authors have adapted the 10 Step framework for military applicability from Philip Kotler, Ned Roberto, and Nancy Lee, *Social Marketing: Improving the Quality of Life*, 2nd ed. (Thousand Oaks: Sage Publications, 2002). The concept of social marketing provides a useful 10 step for designing and evaluating a strategic communications campaign.

[64] U.S. Central Intelligence Agency, "Colombia," The World Fact Book, https://www.cia.gov/library/publications/the-world-factbook/geos/co html (accessed January 8, 2009).

[65] U.S. Army Colonel Jim Marshall, phone interview by author, March 2, 2009. Colonel Marshall advocates duration as a sixth criterion. However, for the purposes of this study, it is included as an aspect of delivery.

[66] Stavridis, 6.

[67] Ibid.

[68] Defense Science Review Board, 11.

information campaign.[69] Adaptability has been cited as one of the primary traits of successful insurgencies; therefore, adaptability needs to be the same trait for any strategic communication campaign designed to shape and counter it.[70]

Context, content, coordination, delivery, and assessment are evaluation tools for analyzing strategic communication. They are not mutually exclusive aspects, so there should be overlapping and interconnectivity among them during planning and evaluation. This set of criteria can be applied to evaluating U.S. strategic communication efforts in campaign planning and as a quality control mechanism during operations. To illustrate how these criteria can be used to evaluate effectiveness, an example of a failed strategic communication endeavor, and its resulting devastating effects, is provided.

An Example of Ineffective Strategic Communication: Disbanding the Iraqi Army

Many agree that Ambassador L. Paul Bremer's disbanding of the Iraqi Army in the wake of the 2003 U.S. invasion was a serious mistake that had strategic implications.[71] The controversial action by the head of the Coalition Provisional Authority (CPA) was also an ineffective attempt at strategic communication, with its failure shaping disastrous and costly consequences for the U.S., its coalition partners, and Iraq. The decision was a strategic communication failure on multiple levels, in particular, context, content, and coordination.

---

[69] Helmus, Paul, and Glenn, vii.

[70] Hammes, 22.

[71] John Keegan, *The Iraq War* (New York: Alfred A. Knopf, 2004), 205. Charles H. Ferguson, *No End in Sight: Iraq's Descent into Chaos* (New York: Public Affairs, 2008), 167. Thomas E. Ricks, *Fiasco: The American Military Adventure in Iraq* (New York: Penguin Group, 2007), 161-165. Michael R. Gordon and Bernard E. Trainor, *Cobra II: The Inside Story of the Invasion and Occupation of Iraq* (New York: Pantheon Books, 2006), 483-485. As expected, Ambassador Bremer defended his decision in his book. L. Paul Bremer and Malcolm McConnell, *My Year in Iraq: The Struggle to Build a Future of Hope* (New York: Simon & Schuster, 2006), 58.

CPA Order #2, signed by Bremer in May 2003, dissolved the Iraqi Defense Ministry and associated organizations and terminated the employment of 385,000 thousand soldiers.[72] Bremer believed the dissolution was necessary to signal the end of Saddam Hussein's rule and reassure excluded Shia and Kurds that the old Sunni Baathist-controlled military apparatus would not return. In a letter to President Bush on May 22, 2003, a day before signing CPA Order #2, Bremer indicated one of his two most important goals was "make it clear to everyone that we mean business: that Saddam and the Baathists are finished," he continues, "I will parallel this step [dissolution of the Baath Party] with an even more robust measure dissolving Saddam's military and intelligence structures to emphasize we mean business."[73] In his book, Bremer reinforced the strategic communication aspect of dissolving the military by writing, "But it would formally dismantle the old power structure and signal that the fall of Saddam and the Baathists was permanent."[74] Regardless of his intentions, the message Bremer sent through his action failed to consider the context and content and was not coordinated with other stakeholder executive agencies.

When analyzed according to context, Bremer's action failed to account for the systemic and interdependent factors surrounding the Iraqi Army and, thus, shaped instability in Iraq. For example, ceasing payment to so many organized, trained, and young soldiers in an environment where there was little employment would prove to be disastrous, fueling resentment for the

---

[72] Ricks, 162.

[73] The letter was provided to the New York Times by Bremer in September, 2007. L. Paul Bremer, "Letter from L. Paul Bremer to George W. Bush, May 22, 2003," *The New York Times*, September 3, 2007, http://www.nytimes.com/ref/washington/04bremer-text1.html?ref=Washington (accessed March 14, 2009).

[74] Bremer and McConnell, 56-57. Another example is given during Bremer's interview with PBS Frontline. He stated, "And we felt it was very important, again, as with the Ba'ath Party, to make the point that the old Iraqi army is never coming back." PBS Frontline, "Truth, War, and Consequences: Interview L. Paul Bremer," *PBS Frontline*, August 1, 2003, http://www.pbs.org/wgbh/pages/frontline/shows/truth/interviews/bremer.html (accessed March 14, 2009).

occupiers.[75] Bremer also failed to understand that the Iraqi Army, not the Saddam's Republican Guard, had been a nationally unifying institution since the 1920's. Its large officer corps, almost 200,000 men, was relatively professional and mistrusted by Saddam.[76] Therefore, Bremer's intended consequence of disbanding a monolithic Baathist entity was not consistent with the context of the situation. From a content perspective, CPA Order #2 also failed to account for the cultural nuances of the audience. According to the edict, The New Iraqi Corps, or NIC as CPA called it, was to replace the disbanded Iraqi Army. *New York Times* Military Correspondent Michael Gordon and retired U.S. Army Lieutenant General Bernard Trainor write, "For all the talk of building Iraqi pride, the name of the new force betrayed a certain cultural insensitivity: NIC, when pronounced, sounded very much like 'f—k' in Arabic. It was a graphic demonstration of just how little the liberators understood the nation they occupied."[77] The strategic communication failure of disbanding the Iraqi Army was also due to the fact it was not coordinated and synchronized across U.S. agencies. The Secretary of State, National Security Advisor, and elements of the DoD, to include the Joint Chiefs of Staff, Central Command, and units on the ground in Iraq, were unaware of the action until it happened. In fact, the message of dissolving the army was opposite to the collaborative work between the Iraqi Army and U.S. military that was already happening on the ground.[78] Therefore, there was little, if any, effective coordination in reducing the "say/do gap" or synchronizing strategic communication activity from the responsible agencies, like the Broadcasting Board of Governors or DoS.

---

[75] Ricks, 162. Supported by Charles Ferguson's 2006 interview with Mahmoud Othman, Kurdish Member of the Iraqi Parliament. Mahmoud stated, "The Iraqi Army, which was disbanded then, they were in the country, gradually, again, they got, uh, organizing themselves, and trying to work underground." Ferguson, 175.

[76] Ferguson, 173. Gordon and Trainor, 485. Ricks, 163.

[77] Gordon and Trainor, 483. It is interesting to note that Bremer does not mention the New Iraqi Corps in his 2006 book, although CPA Order #2 clearly labels it as such. Rather, he refers to it as the New Iraqi Army, or NIA. Bremer and McConnell, 56-58.

[78] Ricks, 161-163. Gordon and Trainor, 483-484. Ferguson, 168.

The effect of Bremer's message and action was disastrous for the U.S. and Iraq. Gordon and Trainor write, "The reaction to Order No. 2 in Iraq was incendiary. The decree prompted angry demonstrations in Baghdad."[79] Pulitzer Prize Winner Thomas Ricks highlights the strategic communication failure by pointing out some demonstrators carried signs that said, "Please Keep Your Promises." In a haunting premonition to the coming insurgency, another protestor vowed, "We are all very well-trained soldiers and we are armed. We will start ambushes, bombings, and even suicide bombings. We will not let the Americans rule us in such a humiliating way."[80] Ultimately, Bremer's intent to signal the end of an era produced another one, that is, an era of costly conflict, in both blood and fortune, for all nations involved. This strategic communication failure illustrates the vital importance of understanding the context of a situation. As a result, it is essential to understand the context of the conflict in Colombia before evaluating U.S. strategic communication efforts to shape stability there.

Context and Future of the Conflict in Colombia

The predominant threat to the stability and security of Colombia is the *Fuerzas Armadas Revolucionarias de Colombia* (FARC), which is a social revolutionary terrorist group that has terrorized the Colombian people and government for almost 45 years.[81] Over the past seven years, the security and domestic policies of Colombian President Álvaro Uribe has drastically negated the FARC's influence and impact. Both through the efforts of the government and the

---

[79] Gordon and Trainor, 484.

[80] Ricks, 164.

[81] Discussing the FARC, Colombian Vice-President Francisco Santos stated, ""terrorist groups, based on the economic power of drug trafficking, constitute a serious threat not to just our country but to the entire Andean and Latin American region." Reuters, "Colombia Says FARC Wanted To Make Radioactive Bomb," Reuters Alert Net, March 4, 2008, http://www.alertnet.org/thenews/newsdesk/L04339901.htm (accessed January 21, 2009).

FARC's own narco-terrorist activities, the Colombian people have isolated themselves from the group. International support has dwindled for the FARC as well. However, this enemy of the Colombian people cannot be easily defeated due to many interdependent factors, including history, ideology, geography, and socio-economic conditions.[82] To shape the long-term decline of the FARC, the solution must remain Colombian, but supported by the U.S. This section discusses the context of the Colombian conflict, including the interdependent factors influencing it, and then addresses the potential future solutions.

Colombia and Latin America, in general, has had revolutionary tendencies dating back to the early 1500's. Guerrilla warfare in Latin America can be traced back to 1519, when peasants fought against the abuses of the Spanish colonizers. Over the next two centuries, this tradition continued as locals fought against the predatory behavior of estate owners and government authorities.[83] In 1780, Tupac Amaru II successfully led a revolt of 80,000 indigenous people in Peru and Bolivia for two years until it was suppressed by the Spanish Army. Although ultimately unsuccessful, Amaru's fight for land reform and indigenous rights helped set the stage for the revolutionary activities inspired and unleashed by the French Revolution. One of the great South American revolutionary leaders, Simón Bolívar, stepped to the forefront in 1811 to lead independence efforts against the Spanish. *El Libertador*, as he is known, is still viewed as a hero for many contemporary Latin Americans.[84]

The revolutionary fervor did not end with independence from Spain as socialist and communist influence took root in the fertile conditions present in the region. With appropriate timing, the communist influence of Karl Marx affected the course of Latin America history in the

---

[82] Revolution has influenced Latin America politics and its population since the sixteenth century. Daniel Castro, ed. *Revolution and Revolutionaries: Guerrilla Movements in Latin America.* Jaguar Books on Latin America 17 (Wilmington: Scholarly Resources, 1999), xv.

[83] Ibid., xvi.

[84] Vanden and Prevost, 43.

1860's. Professors Harry Vanden and Gary Prevost write, "Given the immense poverty and sharp class divisions that have marked Latin American history, it is little wonder that Marxism has excited so much interest and generated so much intellectual and political upheaval…."[85] Starting with the 1910 Mexican Revolution, successive revolutions in Latin American based on socialist and communist ideology met with varying degrees of success. Ultimately, Fidel Castro's Cuban Revolution from 1956-59 became the model guerrilla campaign for other similarly minded communist leaders. A Latin American expert, Professor Daniel Castro, writes, "The Cuban Revolution – and Che Guevara, in particular – added an ideological component to guerrilla warfare. After the Cuban success, it was no longer possible to be a successful *guerrillero* without an ideological foundation, and more often than not a Marxist ideology."[86] Colombia was no different, for the segregation caused by its geographic, social, and economic conditions created the perfect environment for the founding, development, and resilience of a Marxist rebellion.

Colombia's diverse geography provides for "spatial fragmentation" of the people along economic, regional, and cultural lines. With the country's most populated areas separated by mountains, the development of an integrated people and polity was problematic. Professors Frank Safford and Marco Palacios write, "Politically, this dispersion has manifested itself in regional antagonism and local rivalries, expressed in the nineteenth century in civil war and in at least part of the twentieth century in intercommunity violence."[87] As a result, these factors led to more difficulties in extending governance over such a diverse country. The economic success of the twentieth century has somewhat exasperated the problem. They write, "Despite the growth of urban middle classes during the twentieth century, profound social differences still can be observed in a continuing breach between the ideal of citizenship and political equality and the

---

[85] Ibid., 231.

[86] Castro, xviii-xix.

[87] Frank Safford and Marco Palacios, *Colombia: Fragmented Land, Divided Society*, Latin American Histories (New York: Oxford University Press, 2002), ix.

realm of continuing privileges and inequalities before the law and justice of the state."[88] The combination of economic inequality and communist ideology led to peasant struggles over labor and land use demands beginning in the 1920's; subsequently, these would lay the foundation for the founding of the FARC.[89]

Originating from self-defense organizations, the FARC's founding was instigated by nation-wide violence and class and political struggle around the mid-twentieth century. Class and political tensions exploded into a period of violence known as *La Violencia*, from roughly 1948 to 1964. It estimated between 80,000 to 400,000 people were slain during internecine fighting.[90] Sparked by the assassination of a leftist leader in 1948, *La Violencia* forced the peasant self-defense organizations to become more militarized. Given the geographic conditions, the groups established themselves and grew in remote areas south and southeast of Bogotá. In the 1960's, recognizing the existential threat that powerful and popular self-defense organizations posed, the government, then a coalition of Liberals and Conservatives called the National Front, launched a military counterinsurgency offensive against them. In1966, the FARC was established by a conference of self-defense organizations, who agreed upon a political platform of agrarian reform and a strategy of mobile guerrilla war.[91]

Throughout the remainder of the 1960's and 1970's, the FARC focused operations in rural areas, especially where colonization highlighted class distinctions, and held true to its Communist underpinnings. Although its main foundation for membership was the peasantry, amounting to over 70 percent, the FARC had an intellectual, educated core rooted in the precepts of the Colombian Communist Party. Because of its ideological roots, the FARC became an

---

[88] Ibid., x.

[89] Vanden and Prevost, 245.

[90] Safford and Palacios, 345.

[91] Jeremy M. Weinstein, *Inside Rebellion: The Politics of Insurgent Violence*, Cambridge Studies in Comparative Studies (New York: Cambridge University Press, 2007), 288.

attractive choice for peasants, who were excluded from the polity. Stanford University Professor Jeremy Weinstein explains, "Political formation, a process that gave new recruits a sense of agency and possibilities for advancement that did not exist outside of the movement, was central to the participation in the FARC." [92] Professor Marco Palacios from El Colegio de Mexico reinforced the effect ideology had on the FARC by arguing, "The Leninist 'democratic centralism' that the group inherited from the Communist Party and has ruthlessly maintained helps explain why the FARC has been able to maintain a solid unity of command, despite the extraordinary dispersion of its networks and combatants." [93] In addition to the attraction afforded by its ideology to a rural peasantry who were excluded politically, economically, and geographically, FARC rule over its controlled territories was appealing. "The FARC filled a gap of state authority in the communities in which it organized, providing a voice for the peasants and a more legitimate structure of authority." [94] Thus, the FARC's ideological base and positive activities for the peasantry set the conditions for its growth in later periods.

In the 1980's, the FARC experienced significant events that would transform it from an armed force controlled by the Communist Party to a larger and influential independent narco-guerrilla army. In the early 1980's, Colombian government oppression of legal opposition inflated the ranks of the FARC. Then, the FARC's leaders were officially recognized as political protagonists in 1984 by the government in a peace agreement with the revolutionary left. The agreement fell apart as the government murdered thousands of leftists. The FARC then separated from a Communist Party weakened by the purges and later undermined by the collapse of the Soviet Union. [95]

---

[92] Ibid., 289-290.

[93] Marcos Palacios, *Between Legitimacy and Violence: A History of Colombia, 1875-2002*, trans. Richard Stoller (Durham: Duke University Press, 2007), 267.

[94] Weinstein, 290.

[95] Safford and Palacios, 356.

Another important element impacting the FARC in the 1980's was the tremendous growth of coca and poppy cultivation in Colombia. Successful interdiction efforts in neighboring Andean Ridge countries coupled with increasing demand in the United States prompted many peasants to switch from less profitable food and cash crops to coca and poppy cultivation. Increased narco-trafficker activity in areas controlled by the FARC forced the group to police criminal and delinquent activity. The FARC imposed a tax for protection on the peasantry, bringing in up to $100 million a year. The increased participation and financial resources allowed the FARC to double from an estimated 9,000 combatants in 1982 to over 18,000 by 1989.[96] This tremendous growth in size and power would lead to disastrous effects for Colombians in the next decade.

The 1990's were another violent decade for the Colombians as the FARC and other armed rebel groups, such as the *Ejercito de Liberacion Nacional* (ELN) fought against the Colombian government and the paramilitary forces. While this was a high time for FARC influence in Colombia, some experts argue that the rapid expansion of the FARC and its involvement in coca production undermined the ideological fabric of the organization. Professor Weinstein writes, "Grappling with these new responsibilities and managing the infusion of resources sapped valuable attention, resources, and capacity from the political work that was at the core of the FARC's revolutionary model."[97] The allure of financial gain without the counterbalance of education and indoctrination filled the ranks with the type of individuals that were more prone to violence, thus contributing to the group's terrorist activities.[98]

---

[96] Weinstein, 290-291.

[97] Ibid., 294.

[98] Ibid., 292. Thomas A. Marks, Ph.D., Professor of Terrorism, Insurgency, and Counterinsurgency at the National Defense University supports this argument, "Committed ideologically to Marxism-Leninism, FARC had increasingly drifted to a vaguely defined 'Bolivarian' populism that had little appeal in Colombia. Polls consistently found the movement with minimal support or even sympathy." Thomas A. Marks, "A Model Counterinsurgency: Uribe's Colombia (2002-2006) vs FARC," *Military Review* (March-April 2007): 50.

Describing the FARC's transition to a narco-terrorist organization, National Defense University Professor Thomas Marks writes, "It's efforts at armed propaganda had fallen off to nothing after a mid-1980's high, and it was increasingly corrupted by reliance on funding from criminal activity - drugs, kidnapping, and extortion (in that order, perhaps $250 million total)."[99] Regardless of the ideological challenges the group faced, the FARC's increased power throughout the country forced the Colombian President Andres Pastrana to seek a negotiated settlement in 1998. The FARC was granted a demilitarized zone, conceding a large swath of its territory for peace. The FARC, instead, intensified the conflict through main force warfare in the demilitarized zone, continuing terror and guerrilla activities.

In 2002, the election of President Álvaro Uribe Vélez changed the dynamic of the conflict, setting in motion the decline of the FARC, other leftist groups, and right-wing paramilitaries.[100] President Uribe's approach, outlined in his *Democratic Security and Defense Policy*, was to extend governance, security, and development to areas of Colombia that were not under the government's control. The policy was a paradigm shift from negotiating with to confronting the FARC and other narco-terrorist groups.[101] Three of the five listed goals of the policy addressed the challenges posed by the FARC, for example, one was "consolidate state control throughout Colombia to deny sanctuary to terrorists and perpetrators of violence."[102] President Uribe was able to accomplish this through integration of national instruments of power

---

[99] Marks, 49. See also Michael Reid, *Forgotten Continent* (New Haven: Yale University Press, 2007), 258-259.

[100] Like many Colombians impacted by the conflict, President Uribe has a personal stake in the FARC's defeat. His father was murdered by the FARC. Reid, 260.

[101] Marks, 49.

[102] The other four goals of the *Democratic Security and Defense Policy* were the following: "protect the population through the increase of state presence and a reduction in violence; destroy the illegal drug trade in Colombia to eliminate the revenues which finance terrorism and generate corruption and crime; maintain a deterrent military capability as a long-term guarantee of democratic sustainability; and transparently and efficiently manage resources as a means to reform and improve the performance of government." Colombia, "The Uribe Administration's Democratic Security and Defense Policy," Embassy of Colombia, http://www.presidencia.gov.co/sne/visita_bush/documentos/security.pdf (accessed February 5, 2009).

with the Colombian military as the lead.[103] For example, he extended control into ungoverned spaces by increasing the size of the police by 30,000 and stationing them in 150 municipalities, which had previously lacked state authority. He also supplemented guard duties by hiring 20,000 locals on a part-time basis.[104] By most accounts, President Uribe's administration has been successful in achieving its goals over the past seven years, and in particular, precipitating the decline of the FARC and other extremist groups.[105] While the demobilization and decline of the FARC has been substantial, the narco-terrorist group is still a threat. Given the geography, socio-economic conditions, and history of Colombia, gains are reversible and the FARC could again challenge the government's authority.[106]

The future for Colombia and the FARC rests on a Colombian solution. Professor Marks argues that Colombia's solution to the FARC, supported by the U.S., is "both correct and

---

[103] Thomas A. Marks, *Sustainability of Colombian Military/Strategic Support for "Democratic Security,"* Shaping the Regional Security Environment in Latin America Special Series (Carlisle, Strategic Studies Institute, 2005), 7-9.

[104] Reid, 260-261.

[105] "Homicides have dropped by 40%, kidnappings by 83%, and terrorist attacks by 76%. Over 31,000 paramilitary combatants and 10,000 guerrillas – mostly from the FARC and the National Liberation Army (ELN) – have demobilized. FARC guerrillas' top leadership has been disrupted, and the rank and file are deserting." U.S. Department of State, *Colombia: An Opportunity for Lasting Success*, Bureau of Public Affairs (Washington, DC, November 6, 2008). See also the January 2009 L.A. Times interview with Colombian Defense Minister Juan Manuel Santos. He states, "Last year was the best year for the Colombian armed forces in all its history. First, there was political progress in that people mobilized as never before to demonstrate against the FARC. Secondly, the number of demobilized rebels rose to 3,480, the highest level in history. Thirdly, after 44 years of our military not being able to touch the FARC leadership -- the seven-member secretariat -- three of them fell in 2008. Fourth, the spectacular rescue in July [of three U.S. defense contractors, former presidential candidate Ingrid Betancourt and 11 others] was so extraordinary that it created a euphoria and self-confidence in our military, and among all Colombians." Chris Kraul, "Q&A with Colombian Defense Minister Juan Manuel Santos," *Los Angeles Times*, January 9, 2009, http://www.latimes.com/news/printedition/asection/la-fg-santos-qa9-2009jan09,0,6759604.story (accessed January 22, 2009). For more detailed explanation of how President Uribe's policies led to the decline of the FARC, see Marks, 49-64; Reid, 262; Gabriel Marcella, *American Grand Strategy for Latin America in the Age of Resentment* (Carlisle: Strategic Studies Institute, 2007), 37; Peter Deshazo, Tanya Primiani, and Phillip McLean, *Back from the Brink: Evaluating Progress in Colombia, 1999-2007* (Washington, DC: Center for Strategic and International Studies, 2007).

[106] Deshazo, Primiani, and McLean, 52.

sustainable."[107] A 2008 RAND study found that terrorist organizations end in five ways: victory, politics, splintering, policing, or military force. However, the two most common were through the political process or because policing and intelligence caused the arrest or death of key leaders.[108] If the recent achievements of the Uribe administration are the maintained, the FARC's victory is unlikely. According to the RAND study, there is an inverse relationship between the breadth of the terrorist's goals and likelihood of settlement with the government.[109] Unless the FARC adjusts its broad goal of social revolution, a political solution is unlikely as well. A report from the Center for Strategic and International Studies opines on a possible political solution with the FARC, "While neutralized militarily, it is not defeated and will not consent to real peace talks until a point is reached where it no longer has any hope of prevailing over the government. That realization will probably come slowly, enhanced by the increasingly tarnished image of the FARC in international circles."[110] In February 2009, the FARC released hostages in a failed attempt to negotiate for de-militarized zone. These actions could suggest the FARC is reaching such a point where it seeks an acceptable political solution.

Until there is real opportunity for a political solution, Colombia's efforts will, more than likely, continue to be military action but with a greater focus on policing, which is "the use of police and intelligence units to collect information on terrorist groups, penetrate cells, and arrest key members."[111] Regardless of the government's policing activities, it is unlikely for the FARC to be completely defeated given the context behind the conflict. The goal is to continue the FARC's decline, or limit its activities, until the situation becomes self-regulating; in other words,

---

[107] Marks, 64. See also Deshazo, Primiani, and McLean, 53. They write, "While Colombia's accomplishments since the late 1990s are due primarily to the efforts of the Colombian people, the United States played an important support role."

[108] Seth G. Jones and Martin C. Libicki, *How Terrorist Groups End: Lessons for Countering Al Qaida* (Santa Monica: RAND Corporation, 2008), xiii.

[109] Ibid., 78.

[110] Deshazo, Primiani, and McLean, 53.

[111] Jones and Libicki, 11.

the Colombian government is able to continue counterterrorism operations with limited U.S assistance. Ultimately, Colombian public support for the government and isolation from the FARC is a necessity for the policing and political solutions; consequently, effective strategic communication plays a decisive role in either of them. Therefore, the U.S. needs to employ or facilitate effective strategic communication to shape the long-term decline of the FARC.

Applying "Context" Criterion to U.S. Strategic Communication Efforts

The five evaluation criteria for strategic communication account for the entire cycle of operations, from systemic understanding through assessment. Conducting strategic communication is an iterative process that requires routine re-evaluation of the context of the situation. Context is a fundamental criterion for evaluating efforts, for success in strategic communication is contingent on a proper systemic understanding of the situation. For that reason, context is one of the two criteria selected to assess U.S. strategic communication efforts to shape the long-term decline of the FARC.[112]

Analysis of strategic communication activity reveals that U.S. efforts to shape the long-term decline of the FARC are very effective when assessed through the lens of "context." As a reminder, context is concerned with how the communicator has structured the issue and his/her

---

[112] The strategic communication activities of the four most pertinent agencies were evaluated: the Department of Defense, Department of State, the Broadcasting Board of Governors, and The Rendon Group. Within the DoD, the activities, speeches, writings, and documents of the Office of Secretary of Defense, Southern Command , regional component commands, and the military group in Bogotá were assessed. Within the Department of State, the same records of the U.S. Embassy country team and the Undersecretary of Defense for Public Affairs and Public were assessed. Within the Broadcasting Board of Governors, the news broadcasts of Voice of America were assessed. The Rendon Group is a private company contracted by the U.S. government to provide strategic communication guidance and support to U.S. agencies and the Colombian government and military. From The Rendon Group, the author interviewed CEO John Rendon and Latin American analyst Karin Drinkhall. News articles from international media were also assessed.

understanding of the system in which the issue exists. In structuring the issue, U.S. strategic communication efforts, in general, effectively exploit the fact that the FARC is a narco-terrorist organization, terrorizing the Colombian people. The debate is correctly and truthfully structured in a manner that has the Colombians combating self-serving narco-terrorists. In understanding the system, U.S. efforts have correctly identified and stressed that the Colombian government and people have the onus on them to reinforce the FARC's long-term decline. While the conflict affects regional and international stability, it needs a Colombian solution.[113] U.S. efforts are directed at achieving this end through developing, building, and strengthening strategic communication capabilities and efforts of the Colombian government and military. This section explores how the U.S. effectively applies strategic communication to reinforce the long-term decline of the FARC through the lens of context.

Structuring the Issue: The FARC as Terrorists

Structuring the issue so the people and government of Colombia struggle against the onslaught of narco-terrorists frames the debate in such a manner that siding with the latter would be anathema to most. In most of its strategic communications efforts and activities, the U.S. has framed the debate where, truthfully, the FARC has assumed the role of narco-terrorist. Ultimately, this structured debate has contributed to the FARC's domestic and international isolation. The issue was officially structured after the September 11, 2001, attacks when President George W. Bush signed Executive Order 13224, which blocked assets of listed terrorist organizations. The FARC made the list on November 2, 2001.[114] Realizing the disadvantage they

---

[113] Professor Marco Palacios, El Colegio de Mexico, writes, "To win the confidence and compliance of the people, the [Colombian] state must take back its public functions, promote a sense of responsibility among its personnel, and guarantee that basic services-whether supplied by the public or private sector-are delivered to the whole populations." Palacios, 259.

[114] U.S. Department of State, "Comprehensive List of Terrorists and Groups Indentified under Executive Order 13224," Office of the Coordinator for Counterterrorism, http://www.state.gov/s/ct/rls/fs/2001/6531 htm (accessed January 21, 2009).

faced in the structured debate, the FARC's leader Raúl Reyes denounced the U.S. for identifying

them as terrorists.[115] However, the FARC's credibility among its traditional support in Europe

was already beginning to deteriorate with the European Union refusing to issue visas to the

FARC's members in December 2001 and the organization's addition to INTERPOL's terrorist list

in January 2002.[116] Since then, key U.S. leaders and agencies have continued the theme.

The top U.S. military commander for Latin America, Admiral James G. Stavridis,

consistently identifies the FARC as narco-terrorists in his speeches, writings, media interviews,

congressional testimony, and his command's public documents.[117] In one article, Admiral

Stavridis wrote, "One of my main concerns is Colombia and its fight against the narco-terrorist

group *Fuerzas Armadas Revolucionarias de Colombia* (FARC)."[118] Similar sentiment has been

stressed by the top U.S. Army leaders for Latin American in the same venues. In 2004, then

Commander of U.S. Army South, Major General Alfred A. Valenzuela wrote, "The FARC has

---

[115] Yadira Ferrer, "Colombia's FARC Deny 'Terrorist' Label Imposed by US," Inter Press Service, November 8, 2001, http://www.commondreams.org/headlines.shtml?/headlines01/1108-03 htm (accessed January 21, 2009). Reyes is also quoted, "It is a campaign of the war, it is nothing more or less than a form of war. They use it to discredit the revolutionary struggle. This campaign has gained strength from September 11, right? When the twin towers fell in the United States and everyone began talking about terrorism, the Colombian government started calling the FARC and all the revolutionary organizations in Colombia and the world 'terrorists.'" Raúl Reyes, interview by Gary Leech, June 2007, Bogotá, Two Perspectives from the Colombian Left, July 12, 2007, FARC-EP, http://www farc-ejercitodelpueblo.org/?node=2,3102,1 (accessed January 27, 2009).

[116] Rendon, interview.

[117] U.S. Southern Command, "U.S. Southern Command 2008 Posture Statement," http://www.southcom mil/AppsSC/files/0UI0I1204838891.pdf (accessed January 21, 2009); U.S. Southern Command, "Command Strategy 2018: Partnership for the Americas" June, 2008, 15. http://www.southcom mil/AppsSC/files/0UI0I1177092386.pdf (accessed January 21, 2009); Admiral James G. Stavridis, "We're All in This Together," *Americas Quarterly* (Fall 2007): 41, http://www.americasquarterly-digital.org/americasquarterly/fallsample1/?pg=8 (accessed January 21, 2009); Admiral James G. Stavridis, "Foundations of Military Professionalism" (speech presented at the Colombian Senior Enlisted Conference, Bogotá, Colombia, July 22, 2008) http://www.southcom mil/AppsSC/files/0UI0I1219067285.pdf (accessed January 21, 2009).

[118] Stavridis, "We're All in This Together," 41.

evolved from a classic guerrilla group to a terrorist and drug-trafficking organization."[119]

However, the military is not the only agency reinforcing the FARC's identity as narco-terrorist.

Another key person for strategic communication efforts is the U.S. Ambassador to

Bogotá. Although there have been four ambassadors at the post since 2001, all have consistently

reflected the structured issue of narco-terrorists versus the people of Colombia. For example, at a

speech in 2004, then U.S. Ambassador to Colombia William Wood stated, "The enemies of

Colombia all operate against the backdrop of the drug trade. The FARC and the paramilitaries are

key narco-trafficking organizations in Colombia."[120] In 2007, then U.S. Ambassador to Colombia

William Brownfield responded to Venezuelan President Hugo Chavez's demand to remove the

FARC from the terrorism list by commenting to the Colombian press, "The FARC is designated

as a terrorist organization because it behaves like a terrorist organization."[121] Similar consistency

in theme is found in the news articles of the Voice of America, an entity of the Broadcasting

Board of Governors.[122] In fact, Voice of America broadcasts are so pervasive throughout

Colombia that they were praised by former FARC hostages, who listened to them while in

---

[119] U.S. Army Major General Alfred A. Valenzuela and Colonel Victor M. Rosello, "Expanding Roles and Missions in the War on Drugs and Terrorism: El Salvador and Colombia," *Military Review* (March-April 2004), 31.

[120] Ambassador William Wood, "U.S. Support for Colombia's National Strategy for Defense and Democratic Security" (speech at Georgetown University, September 20, 2004) http://www.ciponline.org/colombia/040920wood.htm (accessed January 21, 2009).

[121] AFP, "US Says FARC Need to Change Behavior to Lose Terror Label, AFP, January 15, 2008, http://rawstory.com/news/afp/US_says_FARC_need_to_change_behavio_01152008.html (accessed January 22, 2009).

[122] For multiple examples where FARC is identified as terrorist, see Voice of America News, www.voanews.com. The website describes Voice of America as the following: "The Voice of America, which first went on the air in 1942, is a multimedia international broadcasting service funded by the U.S. government through the Broadcasting Board of Governors. VOA broadcasts more than 1,250 hours of news, information, educational, and cultural programming every week to an estimated worldwide audience of more than 115 million people. Programs are produced in 45 languages." VOA News, "US Freezes Assets of 3 Alleged FARC Representatives," Voice of America, January 14, 2009, http://www.voanews.com/english/2009-01-14-voa64.cfm (accessed January 22, 2009).

captivity.[123] The labeling of the FARC as terrorists has had a tremendous negative impact on the organization.

The FARC identification as narco-terrorists has contributed to a degradation of the group's cause, and its credibility has been undermined domestically and internationally. Ultimately, this label has contributed to its continued isolation from the Colombian population. Counterinsurgency theory explains that a cause is necessary for the success of an insurgency. Counterinsurgency expert David Galula wrote, "The lack of an attractive cause is what restrains a priori apolitical crime syndicate from attempting to assume power, for they realize that only criminals will follow them."[124] The FARC's political platform, or cause, was overshadowed by its drug and terrorist activities. Thus, the FARC lost its legitimacy in the eyes of the Colombian people, driving a wedge between the two.[125]

An example of the FARC's loss of legitimacy comes from Colombia's left. Gustavo Petro Urrego is a Colombian Senator who is a member of the leftist Alternative Democratic Pole political party and former guerrilla in the 19th of April movement.[126] Although Senator Gustavo

---

[123] VOA News, "Former Colombian Hostages Praises VOA Broadcasts," Voice of America, May 16, 2008, http://www.voanews.com/english/About/2008-05-16-colombia-hostage.cfm (accessed January 25, 2009).

[124] Galula, 18. The negatives effect to an insurgency resulting from the lack of a cause is covered under *Organization and Unity* in Bard O'Neill's work. O'Neill, 130.

[125] Dr. Ray Walser, Senior Policy Analyst for Latin America at the Heritage Foundation writes, "The FARC is also isolated from political support, with approximately 97 percent of Colombians opposing the organization." Ray Walser, "Colombia v. Venezuela: An Endgame for the FARC?" WebMemo 1986, Heritage Foundation, 2 (July 11, 2008). http://www.heritage.org/Research/LatinAmerica/upload/wm_1986.pdf (accessed January 22, 2009). See also Semana.com, "For decades, the FARC was drunk with blood and gunpowder. They attacked villages, assassinated politicians, kidnapped civilians and opted for the path of clandestine organizations. They made the language of the bullet their only language for being heard, while at the same time, were deaf towards the clamors for truce that governments and the country as a whole made." Semana.com International, "The FARC: Why are they freeing their hostages?" *Semana*, January 31, 2009, http://www.semana.com/noticias-print-edition/the-farc-why-are-they-freeing-their-hostages/120320.aspx (accessed February 5, 2009).

[126] Polo Democratico Alternativo. "Gustavo Petro ¿Quién es?" http://www.polodemocratico.net/Quien-es (accessed January 27, 2009).

Petro has opposed the Uribe administration and is a leftist, he is also a vocal critic of the FARC.

Senator Gustavo Petro describes how the FARC lost legitimacy due to its drug involvement:

> This caused changes in the attitude of the FARC, from being peasant guerrillas, revolutionaries of the old form; they became an army…that grew because they could buy weapons and pay soldiers and mercenaries, and become militarily powerful….but in another way they lost, because their political ideology and their methods grew increasingly distant from society. They became more barbarous, carrying out actions that didn't even target the army but targeted the society in its entirety. They became *isolated* [emphasis added]….Today, they are simply criminals.[127]

Summarizing the view of many experts on the issue, Senator Petro's quote provides evidence that the FARC's narcotics and terrorist activities led to its domestic isolation.[128] Accordingly, the terrorist label applied by the U.S., endorsed by Colombians, and consistently used by both governments in strategic communication efforts has contributed to the FARC's isolation from the people.

A good example of how the terrorist label is degrading the FARC's image and eroding public support is evident in the 2008 mass marches against the organization. Inspired by a Facebook group established by a Colombian engineer, Oscar Morales, the February 4, 2008 march rallied over one million Colombians in cities throughout the country and smaller ones in cities around the world against the FARC.[129] Describing the group as terrorists, Morales wrote:

> Kidnapping is the worst of acts against human dignity, and FARC have kidnapped and kept captive thousands of people over the last years, while they keep growing their drug

---

[127] Senator Gustavo Petro Urrego, interview by Gary Leech, June 2007, Bogotá, Two Perspectives from the Colombian Left, July 12, 2007, FARC-EP, http://www.farc-ejercitodelpueblo.org/?node=2,3102,1 (accessed January 27, 2009).

[128] Supported by Post, 157-158. Weinstein, 292. Safford and Palacios, 364. Boris Saavedra, "Confronting Terrorism in Latin America," in *The Ideological War on Terror: Worldwide Strategies for Counter-terrorism,* ed. Anne Aldis and Graeme P. Herd (New York: Routledge, 2007), 191.

[129] The Economist, "Facing Down the FARC: Public Sentiment Turns Against the Hostage Takers," *The Economist* (February 2008), http://www.economist.com/world/americas/displaystory.cfm?story_id=10650741 (accessed January 22, 2009). Another source estimated that as many as 12 million people marched in 190 cities around the world. Howcast Media, "Facebook, Google, YouTube, MTV, Howcast, Columbia Law School and the U.S. Department of State Convene the Alliance of Youth Movements Summit," Howcast Media, November 18, 2008, http://info.howcast.com/press/releases/facebook-google-youtube-mtv-howcast-columbia (accessed February 3, 2009).

production and drug traffic business, perpetrating all kinds of crimes and *terrorist attacks against people* [emphasis added], bringing poverty and misery to our country, which has suffered this plague and humanitarian tragedy for more than forty years now....Let's commit ourselves to join a million voices in this group so we can make a difference, and let the entire world know that we don't need that "People's Army" here in Colombia; *that FARC is a terrorist group, led by murderers and enemies of the Colombian and World's People* [emphasis added].[130]

Through protest and collective action, the Colombian people are isolating themselves from the FARC and aligning with the government, which is essential to the FARC's long-term decline.[131] The Colombian Defense Minister Juan Manuel Santos confirmed the FARC's continued loss of public support in 2008 by saying, "there was political progress in that people mobilized as never before to demonstrate against the FARC."[132] This year, online Colombian newspaper *Semana* summarized the population's sentiment toward the FARC, "Before the eyes of Colombia they are seen as a terrorist group that has only achieved a bloodbath in which terror is their only source of power."[133] Further evidence for how strategic communication efforts have shaped the conflict is evident in the FARC's consistent denial of the terrorist label.

Since the U.S. identified the FARC as terrorists, the group has consistently and vehemently denied the application of the term.[134] The FARC denied the use of the term as soon it was applied by the U.S. in 2001. Since then, there have been other examples where the FARC has spoken out against it. When asked why some claim the FARC is nothing more than a criminal

---

[130] Comment posted on Facebook, "One Million Voices Against FARC," http://www.facebook.com/pages/One-million-voices-against-FARC/10780185890 (accessed January 22, 2009).

[131] The Economist, "Facing Down the FARC."

[132] Chris Kraul, "Q&A with Colombian Defense Minister Juan Manuel Santos," *Los Angeles Times*, January 9, 2009, http://www.latimes.com/news/printedition/asection/la-fg-santos-qa9-2009jan09,0,6759604.story (accessed January 22, 2009).

[133] Semana.com International, "The FARC: Why are they freeing their hostages?" *Semana*, January 31, 2009, http://www.semana.com/noticias-print-edition/the-farc-why-are-they-freeing-their-hostages/120320.aspx (accessed February 5, 2009).

[134] "FARC members claim that they do not want to be thought of simply as terrorists who work outside of the law." Post, 157.

organization, the late FARC Commander, Raúl Reyes commented, "It is a campaign of the war, it is nothing more or less than a form of war. They use it to discredit the revolutionary struggle....When the twin towers fell in the United States and everyone began talking about terrorism, the Colombian government started calling the FARC and all the revolutionary organizations in Colombia and the world 'terrorists.'"[135] Another example was the FARC's plea to the European Union, a region where they found some support prior to being designated a terrorist organization in 2002. The FARC's website states, "At these particular times it is a necessity that the international community analyzes the qualification of the FARC as a 'terrorist' organization. The inclusion in this 'list' was done by pressure of the first terrorist state of the world, the United States. And this does not agree with reality. The European Union, specially, must look at this objectively - to reconsider its position with respect to the FARC."[136] The pleas failed, for the FARC remains on the European Union's list of terrorist organizations, further adding to the discourse on the subject.[137]

Measuring the success of U.S. efforts to shape the discourse can be illuminated by the Richard Jackson, Lecturer at the University of Manchester. He writes, "At a deeper level, a discourse can be considered successful when its words, language, assumptions and viewpoints are adopted and employed uncritically in political discourse by opposition politicians, the media, social institutions, and ordinary citizens."[138] Given Jackson's criteria, U.S. strategic communication efforts to identify the FARC as terrorists are successful. The FARC's identity as a

---

[135] Raúl Reyes, interview by Gary Leech, June 2007, Bogotá, Two Perspectives from the Colombian Left, July 12, 2007, FARC-EP, http://www.farc-ejercitodelpueblo.org/?node=2,3102,1 (accessed January 27, 2009).

[136] Allende La Paz, "Are the FARC terrorist?" Fuerzas Armadas Revolucionarias de Colombia-Ejército de Pueblo, http://www.farc-ejercitodelpueblo.org/?node=2,3104,1 (accessed January 27, 2009).

[137] EU Foreign Policy Chief, Javier Solona stated, "The answer is no. There is no reason to change our position." BBC News, "EU to Keep FARC on 'Terror List,'" BBC News Online, January 22, 2008, http://news.bbc.co.uk/nolpda/ifs_news/hi/newsid_7203000/7203206.stm (accessed January 27, 2009).

[138] Richard Jackson, *Writing the War on Terrorism: Language, Politics, and Counter-terrorism* (Manchester: Manchester University Press, 2005), 159.

terrorist organization is evident in the discourse of the Colombian people, media, government, and opposition officials such as Senator Petro. It is also evident in the international media and institutions, and there is proof in the FARC's propaganda, itself. Reducing popular support for the FARC as a consequence of structuring the issue of the self-serving narco-terrorists against the people is only one way the U.S. is effectively using strategic communication to shape the long-term decline of the FARC. From a context perspective, it is evident that U.S. understanding of the system is also leading to the desired effect.

Leveraging the System: Supporting the Colombian Solution

The other aspect of context is leveraging a systemic understanding of the issue, and U.S. strategic communications efforts are effective according to this criterion in shaping the long-term decline of the FARC. In particular, the U.S. understands the system requires a Colombian solution.[139] U.S. Army Colonel Timothy Hodge, the Assistant Army Defense Attaché to Colombia explains the requirement of a local solution, "We can influence, but it is up to Colombia to defeat its enemies."[140] Essentially, there is an obvious issue of sovereignty, which precludes excessive U.S. involvement. Recognizing the effects of this interdependent part on the system and the unintended negative consequences of over-involvement, the U.S. has worked to encourage the Colombian solution directly and indirectly through Plan Colombia. However, the improvement of strategic communication capabilities is another necessary method employed, one that is noted as a shortfall by the Colombians. Recommending adjustments to Colombia's National Security Strategy, Colombian Army Colonel Alberto Mejia observes, "Designing and implementing a better and far more aggressive strategic communications campaign must become

---

[139] Professor Thomas A. Marks argues that Colombia's solution to the FARC, directly and indirectly supported by the U.S., is "both correct and sustainable." Marks, 64.

[140] U.S. Army Colonel Timothy Hodge, Assistant Army Attaché to Colombia, email to author, September 24, 2009.

a *government's top priority* [emphasis added]. A special organization or institution must be in charge of guarantying the unity, clarity and aim of all of the 'informational efforts.'"[141] Accordingly, U.S. efforts to develop, build, and strengthen strategic communication capabilities of the Colombian government and military have been effective.

One method of empowering the Colombian solution is the work of The Rendon Group, who is contracted by the U.S. government. The Rendon Group supports the Colombian Ministry of Defense with a team of native Colombian advisors. The team's purpose is to support the Colombian government's strategic communication efforts abroad and to a limited extent within Colombia. Abroad, the goal is to improve the Colombian government's influence, mainly in Europe but also in the region, Asia, and Africa.[142] It is a "multi-pronged" approach that emphasizes Colombia's leadership in the region, the Colombian Defense Ministry as a leader in counterinsurgency, and most importantly, degrades the image of the FARC.[143] Other U.S. executive agencies also work to empower the Colombian solution.

The U.S. Military Group in Colombia works towards building the government's strategic communication capabilities. The Military Group is Southern Command's representative to the U.S. ambassador, liaison to the Colombian military, and oversees most U.S. military activities and deployments in the country.[144] Arier Santiago, Strategic Communication Officer in the Military Group, explains their efforts:

> MILGRP [Military Group] Colombia has invested considerable efforts during the last six years in building COLMIL [Colombian Military] and COLGOV [Colombian Government] communication capabilities. After training seminars, specialized crisis

---

[141] Colombian Army Colonel Alberto Mejia, "Colombia's National Security Strategy, A New 'COIN' Approach," (Strategy Research Project, U.S. Army War College, 2008), 30.

[142] U.S. population and government is not the target of The Rendon Group's influence campaigns. By law, it cannot be.

[143] Karin Drinkhall, Strategist, The Rendon Group, phone interview by author, November 10, 2008.

[144] U.S. Southern Command, "U.S. Southern Command Organization," U.S. Southern Command, http://www.southcom.mil/PA/Facts/CmdOrg.htm (accessed February 2, 2009).

management coordination, international exchanges and many communication Mil-to-Mil engagements combined with equipment at the proper echelons, we can see COLGOV and COLMIL success in improved communication capabilities.[145]

The Rendon Group and Military Group efforts have empowered the Colombian government to be more successful in their endeavor to promote their policies. Remarking on the success, Professor Marks writes, "*Democratic Security* covers all bases: comic books, cartoon shows, a website, school appearances, and other psyop [psychological operations] products have been deployed to win over Colombia's newest generation."[146] However, not all of U.S. efforts to leverage a Colombian solution have been through building strategic communication capacity; some efforts are more direct.

Consistent with the concept of the Colombian solution, the U.S. Undersecretary of State for Public Diplomacy and Public Affairs seized on the opportunity created by the Colombian inspired and led mass marches against the FARC. Partnering with Facebook, Google, YouTube, MTV, Howcast, and Columbia Law School, the DoS hosted a conference in New York designed to form a global youth movement against terrorism based on the inspiration of Colombia's Oscar Morales and "One Million Voices Against the FARC." The goal of the newly formed Alliance of Youth Movements was to produce a manual and online hub for youth to use new media to combat violence and oppression.[147] Oscar Morales, the Colombian founder of the mass movement against the FARC, spoke at the conference and was honored by internationally recognized celebrities and media. Thus, a key node in the U.S. strategic communication network, then

---

[145] Arier Santiago, Information Operations and Strategic Communication, Military Group, U.S. Southern Command, Bogotá, Colombia, email to author, November 26, 2008.

[146] Thomas A. Marks, "A Model Counterinsurgency: Uribe's Colombia (2002-2006) vs FARC," *Military Review* (March-April 2007): 60.

[147] Howcast Media, "Facebook, Google, YouTube, MTV, Howcast, Columbia Law School and the U.S. Department of State Convene the Alliance of Youth Movements Summit," Howcast Media, November 18, 2008, http://info.howcast.com/press/releases/facebook-google-youtube-mtv-howcast-columbia (accessed February 3, 2009).

Undersecretary of State for Public Diplomacy and Public Affairs James K. Glassman, was able to highlight the Colombian people's solution internationally.

When evaluated according to the criterion "context," it is evident that U.S. strategic communication efforts to shape the long-term decline of the FARC have produced documented success and, therefore, are effective. The U.S. was effective in structuring the issue so that the FARC has become known as "terrorists" both in Colombia and internationally. The U.S. was also effective in understanding that the system requires a Colombian solution. In addition, the U.S. effectively acted on that understanding by building and strengthening Colombian strategic communication capacity and by empowering the Colombian's people solution. However, context is only one criterion to analyze strategic communication; coordination is also an important measurement of effectiveness.

Applying "Coordination" Criterion to U.S. Strategic Communication Efforts

Coordination is selected as a criterion in this study due to its vital importance in ensuring effects are maximized and efforts are not wasted or even detrimental when not synchronized. As emphasized in Senator Brownback's definition and described in the DoD's principles, strategic communication must be coordinated and synchronized vertically and horizontally to achieve the synergy of effects.[148] Coordination analysis for this conflict is essential given the variety of U.S. agencies and stakeholders involved in the region and country, for example, the DoD, DoS, and The Rendon Group.

---

[148] *Strategic Communication Act of 2008*, S9283. U.S. Department of Defense, *Principles of Strategic Communication,* Unity of Effort section.

Strategic communication for the conflict in Colombia is not well coordinated at the national level and, therefore, lacks synergy of effects. On the other hand, there seems to be effective integration vertically within the executive branches and horizontally across them at the operational level and below. It also seems there is effective horizontal integration between the U.S. government and its Colombian counterpart, resulting from the collective efforts of the U.S. Southern Command's Military Group in Colombia and The Rendon Group. This horizontal integration seems to continue down through the operational level and to a varying degree as the tactical level. However, besides the application and use of the term "terrorist," there is limited national level focus, prioritization, and synchronization. As a result, while U.S. strategic communication efforts are effective in piecemeal, lack of nationally coordinated messaging and action lacks a synergistic effect. This section discusses U.S. strategic communication efforts to shape the long-term decline of the FARC according to coordination.

While there has been increased interagency strategic communication cooperation within the past few years, the lack of an institutionalized nationally coordinating strategic communication entity limits the synergy of effects for a particular region or country.[149] Some communications and foreign relations experts understand this requirement and highlight the limiting effect the lack of such an entity has on U.S. strategic communication efforts specific to a region or country.[150] National level synchronization occurs at the National Security Council,

---

[149] Evidence for the increase in interagency cooperation comes from U.S. Army Lieutenant Colonel Josslyn Aberle, Lead Strategic Planner, Office of the Secretary of Defense, Joint Communications, phone interview by author, December 2, 2008. LTC Aberle stated interagency strategic communication coordination has improved "leaps and bounds" since 2006. She remarked, "Everything we do is interagency with the State Department." According to LTC Aberle, there are weekly National Security Council Policy Coordinating Committee (PCC) meetings on strategic communication with additional weekly sub-PCC meetings "worker bees" on Iraq and Afghanistan. In addition, there is personnel exchange with the DoS's Global Strategic Engagement Committee. Finally, she stated the Office of Secretary of Defense , DoS and the Broadcasting Board of Governors collaborate on Afghanistan during meetings called the "Afghan Deep Dive."

[150] See Foreign Affairs Council, 20. Bruce Gregory, "Public Diplomacy and National Security: Lessons from the U.S. Experience," *Small Wars Journal* (August 2008), under "Leverage knowledge, skills, and creativity in civil society," http://smallwarsjournal.com/mag/2008/08/public-diplomacy-and-

which coordinates the activities of the DoD, DoS, and Broadcasting Board of Governors. The 2007 National Strategy for Public Diplomacy and Strategic Communication is the document meant to answer the coordinating shortfall. It is a broad strategy; thus, it is not region or country-specific.[151] At this level, a coordinating document is necessary to synchronize all national strategic communication specific to an area, especially one as critical as Colombia. At the national level, no such strategic communication specific document seems to exist. For example, there is no National Plan for Strategic Communication, which could guide the collective activities of the U.S. in Colombia.[152] A National Center for Strategic Communication could be the governmental entity to produce such a vital coordinating and synchronizing document. Not having a guiding document coordinating communication programs, including setting the context and content, where the U.S. national interest is at stake is a serious problem, especially in today's information environment.

In addition to a lack of a strategic communication-focused document for the region, key nationally coordinating documents for the area often fail to address this decisive enabler. One example is found in the 2009 National Drug Control Strategy, proposed by President George W. Bush in February 2008. With 90 percent of the cocaine consumed in the United States originating in Colombia, the 2009 National Drug Control Policy is an important document governing U.S. activities there.[153] The document does not, however, mention public diplomacy as an employed

---

national.php (accessed February 6, 2009). Strategic Communication Act of 2008, S 3546, 110th Cong., Congressional Record (September 23, 2008): S9284.

[151] U.S. National Security Council, *U.S. National Strategy for Public Diplomacy and Strategic Communication,* Strategic Communication and Public Diplomacy Policy Coordinating Committee (Washington, DC: 2007).

[152] Aberle, interview. Contrary to the author's argument that there is a requirement for a national level coordinating document, LTC Aberle does not believe one should exist. According to LTC Aberle, such a document would lead to micro-management and lack of resources and focus exists for organizing one.

[153] Simon Romero, "Cocaine Sustains War in Rural Colombia," *New York Times*, July 27, 2008, http://www.nytimes.com/2008/07/27/world/americas/27colombia.html?8br (accessed February 1, 2009).

method in the Andean Counterdrug Program. On the other hand, public diplomacy is listed as something the U.S. will assist the Afghanistan government in the section for Afghan Counterdrug Support. It is not an issue of lack of funds, for the Andean Counterdrug Program, $601.9 million, is almost double the amount than the one in Afghanistan.[154] Rather, it is an indicator of strategic communication's lower priority, which ultimately results in lower synergy of U.S. efforts. However, as one moves vertically down the chain of authority into the executive branch, more coordination and synchronization is conducted.

Moving down a level to the executive agency headquarters level, related documents can be found on strategic communication but, unfortunately, there is not one specific to Colombia. Country-specific documents do exist, for there is one for Afghanistan. The Deputy Secretary of Defense Gordon England issued a strategic communication plan for Afghanistan in 2007 that clearly defines the purpose, end state, audiences, themes, tools and enablers, and assessment.[155] With the diversity of DoD units and assets conducting and supporting operations in Afghanistan, coordinating guidance is needed. Although the requirements for the DoD are less in Colombia than in Afghanistan, Colombia's regional importance warrants such a coordinating document. At the DoD level, one does not exist.[156] Progression down the chain of authority, for example the combatant command level for the military, reveals more area focused planning and coordination.

The command emphasis accorded to strategic communication by U.S. Southern Command Commander, Admiral Stavridis, leads to an intense focus on its planning, coordination, and execution. Three key documents, two of which are strategic communication-focused, provide overarching guidance and direction for the command and its subordinate units. The first is the

---

[154] White House, *National Drug Control Strategy: FY 2009 Budget Summary*, (Washington, DC: February 2008), 5.

[155] U.S. Department of Defense, *Strategic Communication Plan for Afghanistan*, (Washington, DC: September 2007).

[156] Aberle, interview.

Command Strategy 2018, which provides context, including challenges such as terrorism, and the ends, ways, and means for U.S. Southern Command's area of operations.[157] The first of the strategic communication-specific command documents is the *Strategic Communication Framework*. The purpose of this 2006 document is two-fold. First, it provides overarching strategic communication guidance. Recognizing the importance of a coordinated effort, the second purpose is "to enhance organizational effectiveness by advancing consistent, seamless messages to USSOUTHCOM audiences in order to generate support for the command's mission and objectives."[158] The document provides the command's vision, objectives, communication construct, themes, and key audiences and messages.

The second and more recent document, *Strategic Communication Plan for Fiscal Year 2009*, builds on both the command strategy and strategic communication framework and ultimately acts as the coordinating and synchronizing policy. The purpose of this more execution-oriented document is to "provide principles and objectives to create and *synchronize* [emphasis added] an effective coordination plan for the entire USSOUTHCOM-enterprise and provide guidance to component and joint task force commanders to develop their *supporting* [emphasis added] communication plans for FY 09."[159] Besides identifying objectives and metrics for assessment, the strategic communication plan also details format and time requirements as a feedback mechanism to the command. The coordination and synchronization organized by U.S. Southern Command allows for synergistic effects of strategic communication activities for units and individuals within its authority.

---

[157] U.S. Southern Command, *U.S. Southern Command Strategy 2018: Partnership for the Americas" June, 2008*, http://www.southcom.mil/AppsSC/files/0UI0I1177092386.pdf (accessed January 21, 2009).

[158] U.S. Southern Command, *U.S. Southern Command Strategic Communication Framework*, Policy Memorandum 16-06 (Miami, December 19, 2006), 1.

[159] U.S. Southern Command, *U.S. Southern Command Enterprise Strategic Communication Plan for FY 09* (Miami, October 20, 2008), 1.

An example of the coordination resulting from Southern Command's strategic communication framework and communication plan is evident in the activities of its subordinate unit, the U.S. Military Group in Colombia. The Military Group effectively bases its strategic communication efforts on Southern Command guidance. Arier Santiago, Strategic Communication Officer in the Military Group, describes vertical and horizontal coordination and synchronization resulting from their process:

> Guidance comes from above and we synchronize efforts….We can consider a regular donation event, like many that occur in Colombia every year. The SOUTHCOM [Southern Command] framework is used as the overall guidance. Events are coordinated and often PA [Public Affairs] guidance is received as needed. PA guidance is in line with strategic themes. Speeches are sometimes drafted and also aligned with the framework. Host nation receives explanation of events which also contains messaging in line with the framework guidance. Depending on the event the themes and messages are coordinated with the COLMIL SC [Colombian Military Strategic Communication] office at the Joint Command or respective level as needed.[160]

Thus, the strategic communication efforts of the Military Group are effectively coordinated within the overarching guidance provided by Southern Command. The resulting effects, according to Mr. Santiago, have contributed to the Colombian's success, including the decline of the FARC. He writes, "Strategic Communication has been a key element in Colombian success for 2008… We can see the key effects of various communication plans. We can see how communication synchronized and aligned with themes and messages has been extremely successful."[161] Another example of vertical and horizontal coordination at the operational level and below is evident by the activities of The Rendon Group.

The Rendon Group, a contracted firm, effectively coordinates its strategic communication efforts horizontally with U.S. Southern Command and the Colombian government and military. The Rendon Group uses Southern Command's strategic communication guidance and framework

---

[160] Arier Santiago, Information Operations and Strategic Communication, Military Group, U.S. Southern Command, Bogotá, Colombia, email to author, November 26, 2008.

[161] Ibid.

for its messaging, ensuring horizontal coordination. There is also effective coordination and collaboration between the two agencies. In addition, the firm supports the Colombian government and military, so The Rendon Group's activities are obviously coordinated and synchronized with them. Finally, the same Rendon Group employees working with the Colombians also coordinate efforts with Arier Santiago, the Strategic Communication Officer of the U.S. Military Group. As a result, there is coordination and synchronization of the U.S. elements and the Colombians in the country.[162] While these efforts at the regional executive agency and below have and continue to produce effective results, there is little coordination, as evidenced above, at the national level.

The synergy resulting from a more centrally-generated approach at a national level would be more effective in shaping the long-term decline of the FARC. Lack of area or country-specific focus on the national level, which could coordinate efforts of all the components of the information instrument, is limiting a synergy of effects. On the other hand, there are remarkably well coordinated and synchronized effects at lower levels. While these coordinated effects are crucial for success, they could fail to achieve a long-term aggregate effect. With piecemeal efforts, there is a limit to the overall shaping effect on the security environment in Colombia and on the long-term decline of the FARC.

Conclusion

The greatest threat to Colombia's stability is the *Fuerzas Armadas Revolucionarias de Colombia* (FARC), a social revolutionary and narco-terrorist group. Although the combined efforts of the Colombian government and people recently reduced the influence and power of the FARC, the context behind the conflict in Colombia suggests the FARC has the ability to once

---

[162] Karin Drinkhall, Strategist, The Rendon Group, email to author, November 13, 2008.

again threaten the stability of the country. Since a stable and democratic Colombia is in our national interest, it is logical to conclude that the long-term decline of the FARC is also in our national interest. Consequently, the Colombian solution requires effective strategic communication to shape the FARC's continued isolation from the people and international community and reinforce support for the Colombian government. Therefore, strategic communication needs to play a crucial role in shaping the long-term decline of the FARC, and the U.S. must continue to support the Colombians through its effective employment.

Strategic communication is "engaging foreign audiences through coordinated and truthful communications programs that create, preserve, or strengthen conditions favorable to the advancement of the national interests of the United States."[163] In today's information age, it is a decisive tool for shaping the security environment to advance U.S. national interests. Strategic communication needs to be employed in an "anticipatory shaping" manner, where a consistent, pervasive, and coordinated process sets the conditions for U.S. interests. Strategic communication should be a function of the routine operations of our government, for example, conducted in the DoD's Shape Phase, or Phase 0. In addition, strategic communication serves as a fundamental consideration during campaign planning and execution during and after major U.S. operations. Finally, results of its effective employment set the stage for long-term peace, which is similar to the FARC's decline in Colombia.

A self-regulating Colombian solution will likely be when the FARC is either limited in its ability to de-stabilize the government and terrorize the people or is incorporated into the political process. Colombia's continued use of military forces and policing will contribute to this solution. These measures alone cannot lead to the solution; rather, the Colombian government must address key socio-economic factors, such as income disparity, political legitimacy, and the

---

[163] *Strategic Communication Act of 2008*, S 3546, 110th Cong., *Congressional Record* (September 23, 2008): S 9283-9284

extension of government authority into areas secluded by Colombia's diverse geography. Regardless, the employment of effective strategic communication is necessary to shape the continued isolation of the FARC by the Colombian people and the international community and to maintain support for the government's policies.

To ensure strategic communication is effective, it can be assessed according to five evaluation criteria: *context, content, coordination, delivery*, and *assessment*. Context is a two-fold requirement. It, first, ensures the communicator has effectively structured the issue to allow for pre-persuasion and, second, checks to see if the communicator has a systemic understanding. Effective strategic communication leverages the communicator's understanding of the system for achieving intended positive consequences and limiting unintended negative ones. The second criterion, content, ensures the communicator conducted a thorough analysis of the audience and created a message which has a meaningful narrative. The third criterion, coordination, ensures the actions and words are coordinated and synchronized vertically and horizontally to achieve a synergistic effect. Delivery, the fourth criterion, ensures that operations and methods employed are based on the context of the environment and are of sufficient duration. Finally, assessment is a necessary criterion because it ensures that the audience's received messages lead to the anticipated and desired consequences. If not, assessment ensures feedback mechanisms allow for necessary re-framing of the context or adjustment to content, coordination, or delivery. Although a prerequisite for success, effective strategic communication must be employed with other lines of effort to influence the complex situation in Colombia.

U.S. strategic communication efforts are effective when evaluated according to the context criterion. First, the U.S. effectively structured the issue in 2001 so the FARC is now commonly known, both in Colombia and internationally, as terrorists. The correct application of the "terrorist" label to the FARC gave the Colombians a way to express their resentment against a former social revolutionary group that now selfishly terrorizes the people. This term allowed the Colombian people and the international community to isolate themselves from the FARC, a requirement for any solution to the conflict. The other aspect of context is systemic understanding, and the U.S. has been effective in that respect by leveraging a Colombian solution. The U.S. has worked to build Colombian strategic communication capabilities at both the government and military level, and resulting operations have been successful. Another example of supporting the Colombian solution was illustrated by U.S. strategic communication efforts to highlight the anti-FARC mass marches to the international community.

According to the coordination criterion, U.S. strategic communication efforts are effective at the regional level and below. However, there should be more synchronization and focus at the national level for synergy of effects. There is effective horizontal coordination and synchronization across the executive agencies, like the DoD and DoS, The Rendon Group, and the Colombian government and military. There is also effective vertical integration within the executive agencies. On the other hand, the lack of a nationally coordinating agency that synchronizes the strategic communication activities of the government, specific to a region or country, limits the synergy, which could be achieved. Given the vital importance of information in the 21st century, national level coordination of strategic communication is essential to effectively shape the security environment.

Recommendations

Based on the observations of U.S. strategic communication efforts to shape the long-term decline of the FARC, the following recommendations are offered. First, the U.S. should continue to label the FARC and similar organizations as terrorists. Even though "War on Terror" is an unpopular and unsuitable term, the correct application of "terrorist" should not be replaced by "insurgent" as some have recently argued.[164] Terrorism is a crime, and the FARC's terrorist activities are crimes against the Colombian people and international community. Labeling the FARC as insurgents gives them a degree of legitimacy, which is wholly underserved due to their narco-trafficking and crimes against the population, such as kidnapping. Therefore, counterterrorism is more effective for correctly labeling what the Colombian government is conducting. This theme should continue throughout U.S. strategic communication efforts, regardless of policy changes.

The U.S. should also continue to support a Colombian solution for the problem. The Colombian solution has been very successful under the leadership of President Uribe. One way is to continue to build Colombian strategic communication capacity, either through the continued efforts of the Military Group, country team, or other executive agencies. However, supporting a Colombian solution should continue beyond building strategic communication alone. U.S. efforts should also involve diplomatic engagements with the Colombian government to maintain its credibility and legitimacy in the eyes of its population. A credible and legitimate government is better equipped in a counterinsurgency and counterterrorist campaign. To maintain its popular status, the Colombian government needs to continue to address the underlying causes of discontent, for example, lack of faith in the rule of law, vast economic disparity, and lack of effective governance. The FARC has the ability to regain ground in a system that historically fosters revolutionary tendencies against illegitimate regimes. Therefore, the strategic communication narrative by the Colombian government needs to be supported by action, with targeted U.S. assistance.

---

[164] RAND researchers Seth Jones and Martin Libnicki recommend that America stop calling it a the "War on Terror" because it creates false expectation of battlefield success and provides jihadist motivation for some. They argue it should be called counterterrorism. Jones and Libicki, xvi-xvii; Richard Jackson suggests that use of the term "War on Terror" dignifies a struggle against a superpower. Jackson, 185.

The U.S. needs to focus on strategic communication training and professional development for members of the DoS, DoD, US Agency for International Development (USAID), Federal Bureau of Investigation, and other executive agencies who are the face of America abroad. For example, strategic communication training is essential for DoD Foreign Area Officers, who serve as defense attachés in U.S. embassies around the world. Besides representing America and communicating U.S. policies through word and deed, Foreign Area Officers are an integral part of the feedback mechanism for assessing strategic communication efforts. Specialized training is necessary to hone these skills. The same is true for other members of the U.S. government serving abroad. Over time, strategic communication-related training and focus can also alleviate the requirement for contracted, outsourced support. Having strategic communication savvy personnel representing the U.S. abroad is a necessity for the information environment.

Congress needs to mandate and appropriate funding for a national-level entity that would synchronize and coordinate strategic communication. The improvements in interagency strategic communication cooperation need to be institutionalized through congressional mandate and, ultimately, secured by appropriated funding. The increase in interagency cooperation is a novel and unstable concept, which has already been disrupted by the change in presidential administrations. While collaboration still exists at the action officer level between DoS and DoD, coordination has slowed considerably and even stalled where appointed positions have been left unfilled for months.[165] When positions are filled, there are the same personal, organizational, and cultural hurdles to overcome to restore collaboration, that is, if cooperation in strategic

---

[165] U.S. Marine Corps Major Matthew Morgan, Plans Officer, Joint Communications, Office of the Secretary of Defense, phone interview by author, March 11, 2009. Maj Morgan has been a Public Affairs Officer for over 12 years and served in Iraq, the Horn of Africa, and Joint Task Force Olympics (2002) in a strategic communication-related capacity. He is also the principal author of the U.S. Marine Corps Strategic Communication Plan (2007) and Task Force 134 (Detainee Operations-Iraq) Strategic Communication Plan (2008).

communication is a priority of the appointed leadership. There have been steps by Congress to mandate collaboration, but such efforts have stalled or fell short. Senator Sam Brownback's *Strategic Communication Act of 2008* stalled in the Senate Foreign Relations Committee and effectively died at the beginning of the new Congress. Senator Brownback plans to re-introduce the bill at some point.[166] The U.S. House of Representatives version of the *Duncan Hunter National Defense Authorization Act for Fiscal Year 2009* contained a provision requiring "the Secretary of Defense to establish a Strategic Communication Management Board to provide interdepartmental and interagency coordination for Department of Defense strategic communication efforts."[167] Unfortunately, the Senate turned down the provision. What passed, however, was the requirement for the President to submit a report to Congress on his strategy for interagency strategic communication and public diplomacy cooperation.[168] While this indicates progress, there is still the requirement for a nationally coordinating and synchronizing entity, as advocated by many leading strategic communication and public diplomacy experts.[169] The DoD, DoS, and Treasury represent the military, diplomatic, and economic instruments of power, respectively. The strategic communication entity would be the principal agent for coordination

---

[166] Phone interview with a Legislative Assistant in Senator Sam Brownback's Washington D.C. Office, March 12, 2009. The name of the interviewee is withheld by mutual agreement.

[167] *Joint Explanatory Statement to accompany S 3001, the Duncan Hunter National Defense Authorization Act for Fiscal Year 2009*, 110th Cong., *Congressional Record* (September 23, 2008): H 8954.

[168] Ibid, H 8953. Recognizing U.S. weakness in strategic communication, the joint explanatory statement adds, "We [Congress] note that numerous studies from independent commissions, the Government Accountability Office, and the Defense Science Board have indicated a lack of clearly articulated strategic goals for the Federal Government's efforts at strategic communication and public diplomacy. Taken as a whole, these studies point to deficiencies in the U.S. approach to this mission that have not been adequately addressed by previous strategies, or any other official government initiative."

[169] In his survey of recommendations and proposals, RAND Corporation researcher, Christopher Paul, indicates that fourteen of the thirty-six documents recommended the creation of a new government agency, like the National Center for Strategic Communication, or a new supporting independent or semi-independent organization, like USA/World Trust by Kristin Lord of the Brookings Institution. The other twenty one recommended a reorganization of the existing machinery, like strategic communication mechanisms in the White House. A common theme among the three options is that there needs to be better coordination. Paul, *Whither Strategic Communication?: A Survey of Current Proposals and Recommendations*, 8-11.

and synchronization of the information instrument of power. Given the decisive role information plays in the 21st century environment, now is the time for the U.S. to formalize and institutionalize its employment of strategic communication.

Finally, if congressional legislation does not result in a nationally coordinating strategic communication entity, the National Security Council needs to delegate that function down to the regional executive agency level. As the activities of U.S. Southern Command suggest, strategic communication can be synchronized vertically and horizontally for synergistic effect. Regional executive agencies, like U.S. Southern Command, have greater capacity and subject matter expertise to effectively design, conduct, and assess a strategic communication campaign specific to their area. One agency in a geographic area should lead the regional-level synchronization and coordination of strategic communication activity, using common themes from the President or National Security Council as guidance. However, the National Security Council would have to ensure the agency is given sufficient authority and appropriate support, financial or otherwise, to accomplish its mission.

Bibliography

Aberle, Josslyn. U.S. Army Lieutenant Colonel. Lead Strategic Planner, Joint Communications, Office of the Secretary of Defense. Phone interview by author. December 2, 2008.

Arcenaux, Craig and David Pion-Berlin. *Transforming Latin America: The International and Domestic Origins of Change.* Pittsburgh: University of Pittsburgh Press, 2005.

Axelrod, David and Michael D. Cohen. *Harnessing Complexity: Organizational Implications of a Scientific Frontier.* New York: Basic Books, 2000.

Bar-Yam,Yaneer. *Making Things Work: Solving Complex Problem.* Cambridge: Knowledge Press, 2004.

Bond, Brian. *The Pursuit of Victory: From Napoleon to Saddam Hussein.* New York: Oxford University Press, 1996.

Bremer, L. Paul and Malcolm McConnell. *My Year in Iraq: The Struggle to Build a Future of Hope.* New York: Simon & Schuster, 2006.

Castro, Daniel, ed. *Revolution and Revolutionaries: Guerrilla Movements in Latin America.* Jaguar Books on Latin America 17. Wilmington: Scholarly Resources, 1999.

Clausewitz, Carl Von. *On War.* Translated and edited by Michael Howard and Peter Paret. Princeton: Princeton University Press, 1976.

Colombia. "The Uribe Administration's Democratic Security and Defense Policy." Embassy of Colombia. http://www.presidencia.gov.co/sne/visita_bush/documentos/security.pdf (accessed February 5, 2009).

Cragin, Kim and Bruce Hoffman. *Arms Trafficking and Colombia.* Santa Monica: RAND, 2003.

Cull, Nicolas J. *The Cold War and the United States Information Agency: American Propaganda and Public Diplomacy, 1945-1989.* New York: Cambridge University Press, 2008.

Deshazo, Peter, Tanya Primiani, and Phillip McLean. *Back from the Brink: Evaluating Progress in Colombia, 1999-2007.* Washington, DC: Center for Strategic and International Studies, 2007).

Dower, John W. *Embracing Defeat: Japan in the Wake of World War II.* New York: W.W. Norton & Company, 1999.

Drinkhall, Karen. Strategist, The Rendon Group. Phone interview by author. November 10, 2008.

The Economist. "Facing Down the FARC: Public Sentiment Turns Against the Hostage Takers." *The Economist* (February 2008), http://www.economist.com/world/americas/displaystory.cfm?story_id=10650741 (accessed January 22, 2009).

Epstein, Susan B. *Public Diplomacy: A Review of Past Recommendations.* CRS Report for Congress. Washington, DC: September 2005.

Ferguson, Charles H. *No End in Sight: Iraq's Descent into Chaos.* New York: Public Affairs, 2008.

Foreign Affairs Council. *Task Force Report: Managing Secretary Rice's State Department: An Independent Assessment.* Washington, DC: June 2007.

Freedman, Lawrence. *Deterrence.* Cambridge: Polity Press, 2004.

Galula, David. *Counterinsurgency Warfare: Theory and Practice.* 1964, Reprint, St. Petersburg: Hailer Publishing, 2005.

Gordon, Michael R. and Bernard E. Trainor. *Cobra II: The Inside Story of the Invasion and Occupation of Iraq.* New York: Pantheon Books, 2006.

Gray, Colin S. *War, Peace, and International Relations: An Introduction to Strategic History.* London: Routledge, 2007.

Gregory, Bruce. "Public Diplomacy and National Security: Lessons from the U.S. Experience." *Small Wars Journal* (August 2008). http://smallwarsjournal.com/mag/2008/08/public-diplomacy-and-national.php (accessed February 6, 2009).

Hammes, Thomas X. "The Message is the Insurgency: Strategic Communications in the Society at War" *Marine Corps Gazette* 91, no. 11 (November 2007), 18-30.

Helmus, Todd, Christopher Paul, and Russell Glenn, *Enlisting Madison Avenue: The Marketing Approach to Earning Popular Support in Theaters of Operation.* Santa Monica: RAND Corporation, 2007.

Huntington, Samuel P. *The Clash of Civilizations and the Remaking of World Order.* New York: Simon & Schuster, 1996.

Jane's Information Group. "Security, Colombia." Jane's Security Sentinel Security Assessment. December 11, 2008. www.janes.com (accessed February 5, 2009).

Jackson, Richard. *Writing the War on Terrorism: Language, Politics, and Counter-terrorism.* Manchester: Manchester University Press, 2005.

Jean, Grace V. "U.S. Must Rethink Military Power." *National Defense* 92, no. 655 (June 2008) 28.

Johnson, Stephen and Helle Dale. *How to Reinvigorate U.S. Public Diplomacy.* Backgrounder #1654. The Heritage Foundation. April 23, 2003. http://www.heritage.org/Research/NationalSecurity/bg1645.cfm (accessed January 2, 2008).

Jones, Seth G. and Martin C. Libicki. *How Terrorist Groups End: Lessons for Countering Al Qaida.* Santa Monica: RAND Corporation, 2008.

Keegan, John. *The Iraq War.* New York: Alfred A. Knopf, 2004.

Kotler, Philip, Ned Roberto, and Nancy Lee. *Social Marketing: Improving the Quality of Life.* 2nd ed. Thousand Oaks: Sage Publications, 2002.

Marcella, Gabriel. *American Grand Strategy for Latin America in the Age of Resentment.* Carlisle: Strategic Studies Institute, 2007.

------. *War Without Borders: The Colombian-Ecuador Crisis of 2008.* Carlisle: Strategic Studies Institute, 2008.

Marks, Thomas A. "A Model Counterinsurgency: Uribe's Colombia (2002-2006) vs FARC." *Military Review* (March-April 2007): 49-64.

------. *Sustainability of Colombian Military/Strategic Support for "Democratic Security."* Shaping the Regional Security Environment in Latin America Special Series. Carlisle, Strategic Studies Institute, 2005.

Marshall, Jim. U.S. Army Colonel. Deputy Director of Strategic Communication, U.S. Southern Command. Phone interview by author. September 24, 2008 and March 2, 2009.

Mejia, Alberto. "Colombia's National Security Strategy, A New 'COIN' Approach." Strategy Research Project, U.S. Army War College, 2008.

Morgan, Matthew. U.S. Marine Corps Major. Plans Officer, Joint Communications, Office of the Secretary of Defense. Phone interview by author. March 11, 2009.

Nye, Joseph S. Jr. *Soft Power: The Means to Succeed in World Politics.* New York: Public Affairs, 2004.

O'Neill, Bard. *Insurgency & Terrorism: From Revolution to Apocalypse.* 2nd ed. Dulles: Potomac Books, 2005.

Palacios, Marcos. *Between Legitimacy and Violence: A History of Colombia, 1875-2002.* Translated by Richard Stoller. Durham: Duke University Press, 2007.

Paul, Christopher. *Whither Strategic Communication?: A Survey of Current Proposals and Recommendations.* Santa Monica: RAND Corporation, 2009.

Payne, Kenneth. "Waging Communication War." *Parameters* 38, no.2 (Summer 2008):37-50.

Polo Democratico Alternativo. "Gustavo Petro ¿Quién es?" http://www.polodemocratico.net/Quien-es (accessed January 27, 2009).

Post, Jerrold M. *The Mind of the Terrorist: The Psychology of Terrorism from the IRA to al-Qaeda.* New York: Palgrave Macmillan, 2007.

Pratkanis, Anthony and Elliot Aronson. *Age of Propaganda: The Everyday Use and Abuse of Persuasion.* New York: W.H. Freeman, 2001.

Rendon, John. Chief Executive Officer, The Rendon Group. Interview by author. Fort Leavenworth, KS, October 13, 2008.

------. "The World, Today and Tomorrow: Past, Present and Future." Lecture, U.S. Army School of Advanced Military Studies, Fort Leavenworth, KS, October 13, 2008.

Reid, Michael. *Forgotten Continent.* New Haven: Yale University Press, 2007.

Ricks, Thomas E. *Fiasco: The American Military Adventure in Iraq.* New York: Penguin Group, 2007.

Ryan, Alex. "Complexity Theory." Lecture, U.S. Army School of Advanced Military Studies, Fort Leavenworth, KS, December 19, 2008.

Ryan, Alex and Daniel Bilusich. "Complicated or Complex?" Unpublished paper, 2007.

Saavedra, Boris. "Confronting Terrorism in Latin America." In *The Ideological War on Terror: Worldwide Strategies for Counter-terrorism,* edited by Anne Aldis and Graeme P. Herd , 191. New York: Routledge, 2007.

Safford, Frank and Marco Palacios. *Colombia: Fragmented Land, Divided Society.* Latin American Histories. New York: Oxford University Press, 2002.

Stavridis, James G. "Foundations of Military Professionalism." Speech, Colombian Senior Enlisted Conference, Bogotá, Colombia, July 22, 2008. http://www.southcom.mil/AppsSC/files/0UI0I1219067285.pdf (accessed January 21, 2009).

------. "We're All in This Together." *Americas Quarterly* (Fall 2007): 41-43. http://www.americasquarterly-digital.org/americasquarterly/fallsample1/?pg=8 (accessed January 21, 2009).

------. "Strategic Communication and National Security." *Joint Force Quarterly,* no. 46 (July, 2007): 4-7.

Thompson, Sir Robert. *Defeating Communist Insurgency: The Lessons of Malaya and Vietnam.* 1966. Reprint, St. Petersburg: Hailer Publishing, 2005.

U.S. Central Intelligence Agency. "Colombia." World Fact Book. https://www.cia.gov/library/publications/the-world-factbook/geos/co.html (accessed January 8, 2009).

U.S. Congress. Congressional Record. 110th Cong., 1st sess., 2007, S 2896.

------. *Joint Explanatory Statement to accompany S 3001, the Duncan Hunter National Defense Authorization Act for Fiscal Year 2009,* 110th Cong., *Congressional Record* (September 23, 2008): H 8954.

------. *Strategic Communication Act of 2008.* S 3546. 110th Cong., *Congressional Record* (September 23, 2008): S 9283-9284.

U.S. Department of Defense. *Joint Publication 5-0, Joint Operation Planning.* Washington, DC: December 2006.

------. *National Defense Strategy.* Washington, D.C: June 2008.

------. *Principles of Strategic Communication.* Washington, DC, August 2008.

------. *Report of the Defense Science Board: Task Force on Strategic Communication.* Washington, D.C., 2008.

------. *Strategic Communication Plan for Afghanistan.* Washington, DC: September 2007.

U.S. Department of the Army. *Field Manual 3-0: Operations.* Washington, D.C.: February 2008.

------. *Field Manual 3-24: Counterinsurgency.* Washington, D.C.: December 2006.

U.S. Department of the Army School of Advanced Military Studies. *Art of Design: Student Text.* Version 1.0. Fort Leavenworth, KS: September 2008.

U.S. Department of State. *Colombia: An Opportunity for Lasting Success.* Bureau of Public Affairs. Washington, DC, November 6, 2008.

------. "Comprehensive List of Terrorists and Groups Indentified under Executive Order 13224." Office of the Coordinator for Counterterrorism. http://www.state.gov/s/ct/rls/fs/2001/6531.htm (accessed January 21, 2009).

U.S. Director of National Intelligence. *Letter from al-Zawahiri to al-Zarqawi.* Press Release. October 11, 2005. http://www.dni.gov/press_releases/20051011_release.htm (accessed October 6, 2008).

U.S. National Security Council. *U.S. National Strategy for Public Diplomacy and Strategic Communication.* Strategic Communication and Public Diplomacy Policy Coordinating Committee. Washington, DC: 2007.

U.S. Southern Command. *Command Strategy 2018: Partnership for the Americas.* June, 2008, http://www.southcom.mil/AppsSC/files/0UI0I1177092386.pdf (accessed January 21, 2009).

------. *Enterprise Strategic Communication Plan for FY 09.* Miami, October 20, 2008.

------. "Organization." http://www.southcom.mil/PA/Facts/CmdOrg.htm (accessed February 2, 2009).

------. *2008 Posture Statement.* http://www.southcom.mil/AppsSC/files/0UI0I1204838891.pdf (accessed January 21, 2009).

------. *Strategic Communication Framework.* Policy Memorandum 16-06. Miami, December 19, 2006.

U.S. White House. *National Drug Control Strategy: FY 2009 Budget Summary.* Washington, DC: February 2008.

Walser, Ray. "Colombia v. Venezuela: An Endgame for the FARC?" WebMemo 1986. Heritage Foundation, 2 (July 11, 2008). http://www.heritage.org/Research/LatinAmerica/upload/wm_1986.pdf (accessed January 22, 2009).

Weinstein, Jeremy M. *Inside Rebellion: The Politics of Insurgent Violence.* Cambridge Studies in Comparative Studies. New York: Cambridge University Press, 2007.

White, Hayden. *The Content of the Form: Narrative Discourse and Historical Representation.* Baltimore: Johns Hopkins University Press, 1987.

Wood, William. "U.S. Support for Colombia's National Strategy for Defense and Democratic Security." Speech, Georgetown University, September 20, 2004. http://www.ciponline.org/colombia/040920wood.htm (accessed January 21, 2009).

Valenzuela, Alfred A. and Victor M. Rosello. "Expanding Roles and Missions in the War on Drugs and Terrorism: El Salvador and Colombia." *Military Review* (March-April 2004), 28-35.

Vanden, Harry E. and Gary Prevost. *Politics of Latin America: The Power Game.* New York: Oxford University Press, 2002.

Zambelis, Chris. "Iraqi Insurgent Media Campaign Targets American Audiences." *Terrorism Focus* 4, no.33 (October 16, 2007).

www.ingramcontent.com/pod-product-compliance
Lightning Source LLC
Chambersburg PA
CBHW081858280526
45789CB00007B/2746